ON THE SIDE OF THE
ANGELS

In this "must read" book, Benedict Rogers and Joseph D'souza tell the story of those suffering slavery in India, genocide in Burma, imprisonment in North Korea, and injustice in many other parts of the world. With passion and conviction, they issue a challenge to today's Church to stand up and speak out.

DAVID ALTON (Lord Alton of Liverpool)

"Let justice roll on like a river, righteousness like a never-failing stream!" The cry of the prophets; the longing of the dispossessed and forgotten; the mission of the church; and the theme of this deeply challenging and compelling book.

STEVE CHALKE, Founder of Oasis Global

Joseph D'Souza is well aware of the predicament of the Dalits, some of the most impoverished, underprivileged people in the world. And convinced as he is that our God is committed to justice and righteousness, he has involved himself deeply in the cause of these people, and equally convinced that our Saviour loves them, he has led a powerful, effective movement taking the gospel, love, and holistic ministry to them.

STUART BRISCOE, Elmbrook Church, Wisconsin

This is a biblical, cutting-edge presentation of truth greatly neglected by many, including me. I am in debt especially to Joseph D'Souza who has been one of my mentors in these great challenges that face all of us. We must see how justice and human rights come together with proclamation and discipleship and this book will help us do just that. Here is a "must read" book and now a "must distribute" book as well.

GEORGE VERWER, founder and former International President,
Operation Mobilization

This book is a call to action for a slumbering bride. To love each other as Christ has loved us is a high calling indeed—one that requires a world-view large enough to act with truth and love. Joseph's words continue to pull all of us towards the only appropriate response, sounding the alarm for love in action. As I read these words, I am aware of the need for change.

JON FOREMAN, lead vocalist of the band Switchfoot

This is a clarion call for all who care about the world's victims of persecution and human rights abuses. Benedict Rogers and Joseph D'souza are to be congratulated for creating both a primer in practical advocacy and a source book of spiritual inspiration. Passionately argued, elegantly written, and compellingly evidenced, *On the Side of the Angels* deserves to become a classic of human rights literature.

JONATHAN AITKEN, author, broadcaster, former UK Cabinet Minister and President of Christian Solidarity Worldwide

This book is entirely a new and remarkably fresh approach to the global process of human rights and socio-spiritual justice based on the biblical discourses and the experience of the church. Dr. Joseph D'Souza and Benedict Rogers have made a path breaking effort in this book. . . . I hope not only Christians and human rights activists but every thinking human being would read this book.

PROF. KANCHA ILAIAH, Osmania University and author of *Buffalo Nationalism*

In their book, Dr Joseph D'Souza and his co-author Benedict Rogers have shown deep insight into the Indian reality and faithfulness to the kingdom values that underpin all human rights work—the emancipation of slaves, the freedom to the Dalits, gender justice, and concern for the unborn. I strongly commend *On the Side of the Angels* for every Seminary and Bible College—Catholic, Episcopal, or Evangelist—as well as for the shoulder bag of Christian Civil society activist.

DR JOHN DAYAL, President, All India Catholic Union

In this seminal resource on mission as advocacy, D'Souza sounds a wake-up call to Christians everywhere to get on the side of the angels and Jesus on behalf of the disenfranchised. He appeals for a change in normative Christian mission understanding to embrace "the Jesus way" as Jesus articulated his own life mission in Luke 4 "to bring freedom to those who are oppressed." Joseph encourages the Christian never to fear to tread where injustice shows up. This is the time and the opportunity to become spirit-led agents of change on behalf of the exploited and broken of our world.

LUIS BUSH, International Facilitator, Transform World Connections

ON THE SIDE OF THE
ANGELS

Justice, Human Rights, and Kingdom Mission

DR. JOSEPH D'SOUZA AND BENEDICT ROGERS

WITH TIMOTHY J. BEALS

Authentic

COLORADO SPRINGS • LONDON • HYDERABAD

Authentic Publishing
We welcome your questions and comments.

USA   1820 Jet Stream Drive, Colorado Springs, CO 80921
      www.authenticbooks.com
UK   9 Holdom Avenue, Bletchley, Milton Keynes, Bucks, MK1 1QR
      www.authenticmedia.co.uk
India Logos Bhavan, Medchal Road, Jeedimetla Village,
      Secunderabad 500 055, A.P.

On the Side of the Angels
ISBN-13: 978-1-932805-70-3
ISBN-10: 1-932805-70-2

Published in association with the literary agency of Credo Communications LLC,
Grand Rapids, MI 49525.

All Scripture quotations, unless otherwise indicated, are taken from the *Holy Bible,
New International Version®*. *NIV®*. Copyright © 1973, 1978, 1984 by International
Bible Society. Used by permission of Zondervan. All rights reserved.

Scripture quotations marked NLT are taken from the *Holy Bible*, New Living
Translation, copyright © 1966. Used by permission of Tyndale House Publishers, Inc.,
Wheaton, Illinois 60189. All rights reserved.

Library of Congress Cataloging-in-Publication Data

D'Souza, Joseph, 1950-
  On the side of the angels : justice, human rights, and kingdom mission / Joseph D'souza and
Benedict Rogers ; with Timothy J. Beals.
    p. cm.
  Includes bibliographical references and index.
  ISBN-13: 978-1-932805-70-3 (pbk. : alk. paper)
  ISBN-10: 1-932805-70-2 (pbk. : alk. paper) 1. Social justice--Religious aspects--Christianity. 2.
Social gospel. 3. Missions. 4. Church work. I. Rogers, Benedict. II. Beals, Tim. III. Title.

  BT738.D75 2007
  261.8--dc22

                              2007020043

Cover design: Paul Lewis
Interior design: Angela Lewis
Editorial team: Timothy J. Beals, KJ Larson

Printed in the United States of America

For our friends among the oppressed and persecuted—
the prisoners of conscience, the dissidents, the exiles, the
refugees, the raped women, the slaves, the child soldiers, the
children in bonded labor and the sex trade, the land mine
victims, the "untouchables," the displaced.

You, my brothers, were called to be free.
But do not use your freedom to indulge the sinful nature;
rather, serve one another in love.

Galatians 5:13

Contents

FOREWORD

In this important book, the authors, passionately committed to serving many of the world's poorest and most oppressed people, present some theological, moral, and practical challenges to aspects of contemporary Christian beliefs and practices.

They insist on the need to move beyond established models of evangelism, mission, and aid. Too often, aid and advocacy organizations have remained compartmentalized as Christians have been reluctant to engage in "politics." Instead, the authors argue convincingly, aid and advocacy are inherently interwoven: the Biblical mandate requires us to speak for the oppressed and also to heal the sick, feed the hungry, and clothe the naked.

As they hid in the house, they prayed—no doubt like Jesus—in anguish. A few hours went by, and all became quiet.

The women cautiously emerged from the house and asked their neighbors what had happened. They were told that the attackers had come as far as the house, but, seeing that it was surrounded by heavily-armed soldiers, they left. But there had never been any soldiers there. Angels, it seems, had guarded the women, saving their lives.

It was an angel that intervened to prevent Joseph from divorcing Mary, advising him in a dream that she had conceived her baby by the Holy Spirit.[14] It was an angel who had earlier informed Mary that she would give birth to a son, whom she was to call Jesus.[15] An angel announced the birth of the Messiah to the shepherds,[16] and a whole host of angels appeared to those shepherds, declaring, "Glory to God in the highest and on earth peace to men on whom his favor rests."[17] In almost all these instances, the angel began with the reassuring words, "Do not be afraid."

Our subtitle—*Christians, Human Rights, and the Kingdom Mission Worldwide*—is a challenge to the church in the twenty-first century. There is too much injustice in our world—injustice that is imposed by individuals or by popular

---

14. Matthew 1:19–21.

15. Luke 1:26–32.

16. Luke 2:8–15.

17. Luke 2:14.

culture or by the state or by an ideological system. Mission is incomplete when it fails to confront injustice.

When using the term *church*, we do not refer to any one denomination or institution in particular. Rather, we use the word as it has been used throughout history, as a reference to the body of Christ. Individual believers, Christian sending organizations, local churches, national and international denominations, lay people, and clergy all have a responsibility to help build the kingdom, and so to work for justice.

In this book, we contend that human rights advocacy should no longer be regarded as secondary to kingdom activity. And to do so we draw extensively on Scripture, as well as on our own combined experiences in India, Burma, East Timor, China, Pakistan, Sri Lanka, and Nagorno Karabakh, and on the stories of friends and colleagues in Brazil, Sudan, North Korea, Nepal, Colombia, Laos, and elsewhere. Justice is a central feature of kingdom mission. This idea is expressed repeatedly in both the Old and the New Testaments, but a passage that sets the tone for this book is Ephesians 5:8–14:

> For you were once darkness, but now you are light in the Lord. Live as children of light (for the fruit of the light consists in all goodness, righteousness [sometimes translated *justice*] and truth) and find out what pleases the Lord. . . . This is why it is said: "Wake up, O sleeper, rise from the dead, and Christ will shine on you."

Chapter One

WHO CARES?

Taking It Personally

———————————————

"The Spirit of the Lord is on me,
because he has anointed me
to preach good news to the poor.
He has sent me to proclaim freedom for the prisoners
and recovery of sight for the blind,
to release the oppressed,
to proclaim the year of the Lord's favor."

LUKE 4:18–19

Many experts agree that the first hundred words of any book, article, presentation, or speech are the most important. If the writer hasn't made his point, or the speaker fails to capture our interest with her message, we won't read—or listen—any further. So just how did Jesus begin his ministry? What was the point he wanted no one to miss?

In Luke 4 we get a clue. During the first address of his public ministry, Jesus made it clear what would direct that ministry. In this chapter he states his life's purpose—his personal mission statement—and he tells exactly whom he has come to serve. Quoting from Isaiah, Jesus says that he came to bring freedom to those who are oppressed. And for the remainder of his earthly ministry, he reached out first and most frequently to people with mental and physical brokenness, spiritual sickness, and economic disadvantage.

If we claim to be Christ's followers, his purpose must inform our own purpose. Whether we stay at home to care for family or go to the office, factory, classroom, or field, we too are called to "proclaim freedom" and to "release the oppressed." So when it comes to justice and mercy for the least, the last, and the lost, who really cares? Jesus does—and so must we.

Near the end of his ministry, Jesus explains not only *who* should care but *how* and *why*. He explained to his followers that when he returns he will "separate the people one from another as a shepherd separates the sheep from the goats." He will call to some, "Come, you who are blessed by my Father; take your inheritance, the kingdom prepared for you since the creation of the world." To whom will he address this invitation? Scripture is clear:

> "For I was hungry and you gave me something to eat, I was thirsty and you gave me something to drink, I was a stranger and you invited me in, I needed clothes and you clothed me, I was sick and you looked after me, I was in prison and you came to visit me."

The righteous, caught by surprise, will ask him, "When did we see you hungry and feed you, or thirsty and give you something to drink? When did we see you a stranger and invite you in, or needing clothes and clothe you? When did we see you sick or in prison and go to visit you?" The King will reply: "Whatever you did for one of the least of these brothers of mine, you did for me." This is the kingdom way—the economics and priority of God himself.

Then Jesus appends an ominous footnote (emphasis added): "Whatever you did *not* do for one of the least of these, you did *not* do for me." Jesus' pointed act of calling the hungry, the naked, the sick, the persecuted, and the victims of injustice "brothers" demonstrates the vision and reality of the kingdom of God as he intended it.[1]

These two announcements in Luke and Matthew provide vivid and revealing bookends for the life and times of Jesus

---

1. See Matthew 25:31–46.

Christ. They share what he set out to do, they explain why he did what he did, and they provide a model—a standard—for those who would follow his example and be called by his name.

In Word *and* Deed

Far too many Christians in the world today are engaged in a mission consisting solely of words, "preaching good news" and "proclaiming freedom." That is a curious departure from the example of the early church, and it seems to be a development of a more modern mission trend, where "verbalizing" the Christian faith is seen as the only way of representing and witnessing to Christ in our world. This despite the fact that Christ himself taught through words *and* actions. The mere utterance of the gospel message has bred a Christian faith without life, a Christian witness without involvement in community, a Christian message without salvation.

We contend that this lopsided emphasis in bringing the "evangel" through words has bred the scandal of the present day televangelism culture, which offers words of prosperity and blessing without the cross, without justice, without sacrifice, without social and personal transformation.

Its spokesmen proclaim a "prosperity gospel," a grotesque distortion of the good news, which teaches that if we are truly following God, we will be materially blessed. The implication of prosperity teaching for those who are suffering material deprivation is that there is something wrong with their faith or relationship with God.

Yet these are profoundly misguided interpretations of the kingdom, completely at odds with Jesus' teachings. Reminiscent of the pharisaic religion of Jesus' day, Christians caught in this worldview inevitably proclaim a form of doctrine without power, and they are condemned by the words of Jesus: "You do not know the Scriptures or the power of God" (Mark 12:24).

Someone once asked the sarcastic question, "What have the Bible and justice got in common?" The answer: *Everything.* Unless and until Christian life and witness actually become involved in individual lives and society, we cannot authentically carry out kingdom mission in this world. When our mission efforts fail to address the serious injustices all around us, evil people and destructive ideologies will step in to exploit the vulnerable.

Caring for the Least, the Last, and the Lost

A kingdom perspective on justice, freedom, and human rights draws on a spiritual dimension lacking in secular perspectives. We believe that there are indeed spiritual forces of darkness at work in this world. In his letter to the Ephesians, the apostle Paul notes that "our struggle is not against flesh and blood, but against the rulers, against the authorities, against the powers of this dark world and against the spiritual forces of evil in the heavenly realms" (6:12). We are engaged in a struggle between good and evil, a theme we will explore in more detail in chapter 3.

Similarly, since we are all created in the image of God and are called explicitly to serve the "poor," the "prisoner," the "blind," and the "oppressed," no one should be considered "unclean" or outside of God's love because of his or her origins. Jesus makes this point clear to the Pharisees when he rebukes them for criticizing the disciples for eating food with "unclean" hands: "Listen to me, everyone, and understand this. Nothing outside a man can make him 'unclean' by going into him. Rather, it is what comes out of a man that makes him (unclean)" (Mark 7:14–15). In Acts 10:28, Peter reports: "God has shown me that I should not call any man impure or unclean."

For over 3,000 years the caste system in India has kept millions of people under the oppressive label of "untouchable." To its shame, for almost 2,000 years, the church in India has itself adopted this caste system, in total contradiction to the message of Jesus Christ. How can a human being be "untouchable" when that person is created in the image of God? How can anyone in the twenty-first century allow for the practice of the caste system?

Jesus' words to the Pharisees serve as a stark reminder for the church today, that portion caught up either in the caste system in India or in social climbing in the West.

Isaiah was right when he prophesied about you hypocrites; as it is written: "These people honor me with their lips, but their hearts are far from me. They worship me in vain; their teachings are but rules taught by men." You have let go of the commands of God and are holding on to the traditions of men.[2]

The spiritual dimension of a kingdom perspective challenges unjust systems, structures, and philosophies that affect the eternal destinies of people. In Matthew's Gospel, Jesus points out that it is possible through the actions of traditions, systems, and structures to limit access to the kingdom, to effectively exclude others from entering: "Woe to you, teachers of the law and Pharisees, you hypocrites! You shut the kingdom of heaven in men's faces. You yourselves do not enter, nor will you let those enter who are trying to" (23:13). This verse applies to the world today in which many in authority and power, both religious and secular, are deliberately seeking to prevent others from entering the kingdom.

The totalitarian governments in China, North Korea, Vietnam, Laos, and Cuba do everything in their power to bind and restrict the church's movements, to fill the established, state-sanctioned church with teaching that is submissive to the government, and to persecute those believers who choose

---

2. Mark 7:6–8.

to affiliate with unregistered churches that preach the gospel without compromise. Similarly, Hindu fundamentalists in India and Buddhist nationalists in Sri Lanka, through violence and through the introduction of anti-conversion laws, seek to prevent people from exercising their religious rights. Islamic extremists in Saudi Arabia, Egypt, Iran, and other parts of the Muslim world do not allow for religious freedom.

As a tragic result of such blatant oppression, millions cannot exercise freedom of conscience and experience the kingdom of God. It is our responsibility to challenge any totalitarian system that impinges on the freedom given to man when he was created in the image of God.

What Difference Does It Make?

Jesus continues his sober warning to the religious community in Matthew 23:23–25:

> Woe to you, teachers of the law and Pharisees, you hypocrites! You give a tenth of your spices—mint, dill and cumin. But you have neglected the more important matters of the law—justice, mercy and faithfulness. You should have practiced the latter, without neglecting the former. . . . Woe to you, teachers of the law and Pharisees, you hypocrites! You clean the outside of the cup

and dish, but inside they are full of greed and self-indulgence.

This is indeed a message for the church today. We deserve to feel the sting of Jesus' corrective and be reminded of his mission—and ours—to preach, to serve, and to act on the side of the angels.

In his book *Night*, an account of the horrors of the Nazi concentration camps, Elie Wiesel recalls an incident that raises some sobering questions:

> Not far from us, flames were leaping up from a ditch, gigantic flames. They were burning something. A lorry drew up at the pit and delivered its load—little children. Babies! Yes, I saw it—saw it with my own eyes . . . those children in the flames. (Is it surprising that I could not sleep after that? Sleep had fled from my eyes). I pinched my face. Was I still alive? Was I still awake? I could not believe it. How could it be possible for them to burn people, children, and for the world to keep silent?[3]

If it is hard enough to believe that the world kept silent, how much more extraordinary is it that the church, the

---

3. Elie Wiesel, *Night*, p. 30.

embodiment of the kingdom of God on earth, did so as well? Does that not lead incredulous people to ask the question, as the psalmist does in Psalm 10, "Why, O LORD, do you stand far off? Why do you hide yourself in times of trouble?" The psalmist paints a picture that is as real today as it was several thousand years ago:

> *In his arrogance the wicked man hunts*
> *down the weak,*
>> *who are caught in the schemes he*
>> *devises . . .*
> *He lies in wait near the villages;*
>> *from ambush he murders the innocent,*
>> *watching in secret for his victims.*
> *He lies in wait like a lion in cover;*
>> *he lies in wait to catch the helpless;*
>> *he catches the helpless and drags them*
>> *off in his net.*
> *His victims are crushed, they collapse;*
>> *they fall under his strength.*
> *He says to himself, "God has forgotten;*
>> *he covers his face and never sees."*[4]

The cry of the church, both in prayer and in action, must echo the psalmist's resounding call, "Arise, LORD! Lift up your hand, O God. Do not forget the helpless." When we seek to penetrate the darkness ourselves, bearing the light of justice,

---

4. Psalm 10:1, 8–11.

we will find that God has not forgotten. He is there already, way ahead of us, making a difference and giving us strength and courage to do the same:

> *But you, O God, do see trouble and grief;*
>   *you consider it to take it in hand.*
> *The victim commits himself to you;*
>   *you are the helper of the fatherless.*
> *Break the arm of the wicked and evil man;*
>   *call him to account for his wickedness*
>   *that would not be found out.*
> *The LORD is King for ever and ever;*
>   *the nations will perish from his land.*
> *You hear, O LORD, the desire of the afflicted;*
>   *you encourage them, and you listen to*
>   *their cry,*
> *defending the fatherless and the oppressed,*
>   *in order that man, who is of the earth,*
>   *may terrify no more.*[5]

A Worldly Church

At the moment, it seems as though the church is too much like the world. We react only after a disaster has occurred—and sometimes not even then. Our media is aroused only by attention-grabbing mass slaughter, and, as a result, only then

---

5. Psalm 10:14–18.

are the church and the world aroused. The daily suffering of the ethnic nationalities in Burma; the efforts of Buddhist nationalists to introduce an anti-conversion law in Sri Lanka; the tyranny in Turkmenistan, Belarus, and Uzbekistan; even the oppression of the Dalits in India go largely unreported.

Instead, it takes a million people displaced in Darfur to get the media working and the world moving on behalf of the Sudanese—and even then, action is slow. Darfur has been described as "the world's worst humanitarian crisis"—and it was only after 30,000 people had been killed that the UN threatened Sudan with sanctions, the US Congress conceded to call it *genocide*, and Britain's best-known aid charities launched a national appeal.

"We know the British public, when they know something can be done, are hugely generous and will respond massively to help the suffering Sudanese in this desperate situation," stated the chief executive of the Disasters Emergency Committee, Brendan Gormley.[6] He is right: People are generous when they are faced with the atrocity of genocide played out before their eyes on their television screens.

But, as W. F. Deedes asks, after 34 villages had been looted or burned in Tawila alone, women and children raped, and the entire population set to fleeing:

---

6. "Charities launch appeal to help millions who fled brutal militia," *Daily Telegraph*, July 19, 2004.

Why was the world so slow to react? Why
has the rescue of these people taken so long?
We're talking of a million displaced people,
700,000 of them in urgent need of food aid,
and 150,000 of those likely to be cut off by
the rains which are starting now. "We need
a thousand more aid workers," a United
Nations source says to me, "and it's very late
in the day."[7]

Human rights as a term can sound lofty, or militant, or
political. But ultimately, for each Christian, it means simply
respecting and promoting the human dignity of our fellow
men and women. It means obeying the greatest commands
to love the Lord our God with all our heart and to love our
neighbor as ourselves.

In another part of the world, an American aid worker
shows us what Christian human rights in action looks like.
As one who founded an organization called the Free Burma
Rangers, which takes teams deep inside Burma to deliver help
and hope to the hundreds of thousands of internally displaced
people, he says:

No one is safe from the terror of the dictators.
We have helped to treat and pray for women

---

7. "Shameful cover-up that prevents charities tackling a catastrophe,"
Daily Telegraph, July 19, 2004.

who have been raped by soldiers of the Burma Army, children who have been shot, parents who saw their children thrown into a fire and many others who have endured evil. We want to be witnesses of God's love to all people in deed and word. The imperative of witness calls us to stand with people in their time of need and witness back to the world that these people count. They too need love and justice and mercy. We love the people of Burma and we want to help them—this is our heart. We believe that oppression is wrong—this is our mind. We go because the people of Burma are God's children and it is right to try to help them and be with them—this is our soul. Our family goes with the help of many people, not to take risks, and not sure how much difference we can make, but we go to be a witness for love.[8]

Will you begin to take it personally, responding as a witness for love? In the following chapters we will explore in greater depth the concept of kingdom mission, the biblical basis for human rights activism, the areas where we need to join forces with others on a common platform, the call to speak out not just for our fellow Christians who are being persecuted for

---

8. Free Burma Rangers, Letter to Supporters, May 2003.

their faith—for *our* faith—but for our fellow human beings, created in the image of God, who are being crushed.

But first, we ask our readers to reflect on this prayer by André Dumas. Make it your own, because the one characteristic that distinguishes a kingdom approach to justice and human rights from the world's approach is that we begin with prayer. Prayer is not the end but the beginning. And without it our efforts are futile. Prayer is the fuel of action.[9]

O God,

> *We are one in solidarity with those who live*
> *in danger and struggle.*
> *Whether near or far, we share their anguish*
> *and their hope.*
> *Teach us to extend our lives beyond*
> *ourselves*
> *And to reach out in sympathy to the frontiers*
> *Where people are suffering and changing*
> *the world.*

> *Make us one in solidarity with the aliens we*
> *ignore,*
> *The deprived we pretend do not exist, the*
> *prisoner we avoid.*
> *God, let solidarity be a new contemporary*
> *word for this community*

---

9. André Dumas, *100 Prieres Possibles.*

*Into which you are constantly summoning
    us.*

*God, purify us in our solidarity with others;
May it be genuine, fruitful, fervent and
    humble.
We ask it in the name of him who was
    resolutely one in solidarity
With abandoned, despised, humankind,
Jesus Christ, your son, our brother.*

Amen

Chapter Two

WHAT'S IT MATTER?

Making the Difference

How many years can a mountain exist
Before it's washed to the sea?
Yes, 'n' how many years can some people exist
Before they're allowed to be free?
Yes, 'n' how many times can a man turn his head,
Pretending he just doesn't see?
The answer, my friend, is blowin' in the wind,
The answer is blowin' in the wind.

BOB DYLAN—BLOWIN' IN THE WIND

We continue with some stories—stories of trauma and heartache, individual incidents and widespread terror. These are stories without clear endings, raising questions without easy answers. But the stories must be told and the questions must be asked if we are to reach for answers and learn together how to put our faith into action.

* * *

"My mother—dead," reported Amil, the 15-year-old street boy standing outside a guest house in Dili, East Timor. He drew his index finger down his stomach and demonstrated the action of pulling out his intestines. "My mother, with baby," he added in broken English, before pausing as his eyes filled with tears. "Both dead," he continued.

"My father dead, too," he went on, indicating a thrusting movement of a spear going through his stomach. "And my big brother, too." He explained that his brother's attackers had burned both sides of his face with cigarette butts and hacked off his arms and legs with machetes.

Amil stood there, three months after the terrible eruption of violence that had torn apart East Timor following a referendum on the country's future. The boy, who had witnessed these atrocities with his own eyes, had been left orphaned and destitute. But he was not alone. Thousands of other East Timorese men, women, and children carry similar burdens of pain and trauma—not only from the specific horrors of 1999, but from twenty-four years of brutal occupation.

The question follows: When the men of East Timor were being tortured, when the women were being raped, when the children were being orphaned, and when hundreds of thousands were being slaughtered, where were we? Were we aware that this had happened or could happen?

When the Burma Army captured a 31-year-old Karenni man and held him for ten days, torturing him by rolling logs up and down his shins for hours until his skin had worn down to the bone, pouring water down his throat until his stomach swelled, and then stamping on his stomach until he vomited, where was the body of Christ?

When six Brazilian police officers opened fire on a group of street children who were sleeping in doorways opposite the Candelaria Church in Rio de Janeiro, where were Christ's representatives on earth?[1]

When a group of thugs captured a young Brazilian prostitute and gang-raped and then killed her, gouging out her eyes, ripping out her heart, and throwing her into the sea, where were Christ's followers?[2]

When the homes of India's Dalits were attacked and burned down in Kalapatti Village in southern India by a gang

---

1. *The Streets Run Red with Blood*, Lord Alton, *Just Right*, Issue 10, Spring 2004.

2. Ibid.

of 200 armed thugs, where was the softening force of Christian love?[3]

When the Peruvian police were applying electric shocks to Julio Cusihuaman's eyebrows, temples, cheeks, chest, fingers, toes, and genitals, and then pushing his head into a toilet full of human excrement, where were we?[4]

In his testimony in *Tried by Fire*, Wuille Figueroa, another inmate from Peru, writes:

> Spending the night in Dincote is like staying in a castle of terror. Men and women are taken out of their cells after midnight, a dark hour when lawyers, public prosecutors and human rights representatives do not exist. This is an hour of macabre clamour, of confusing noises, beatings, cries of fright and pain and deep sighs that are lost among the cold and dismal cell walls. They were the cries of the prisoners, the broken images of God who were being tortured.[5]

Those cries reverberate around the world. "Were you there when they crucified my Lord?" many Christians intone

---

3. Asian Center for the Progress of Peoples, June 29, 2004.

4. Anna Lee Stangl (Editor), *Tried by Fire*, p. 148.

5. Ibid., p. 129.

in poignant strains during the Lenten season. But more to the point, as Christ's ambassadors on earth, are we there when our Lord is "crucified" anew, again and again, as he joins vicariously in the suffering everywhere around us?

* * *

Across the globe injustices occur every day. Sometimes they are violent and brutal, in other instances discriminatory and restrictive. They may be political, economic, social, or religious. In some cases people are imprisoned or killed for their faith. In other instances they are jailed because they have stood up against injustice or for freedom. Sometimes the abuses seem trivial, while in other cases they are appalling.

Sometimes violations involve just one individual; in other situations they affect millions. Sometimes they darken the television screens and newspapers of the free world, but all too often they go unnoticed. Sometimes churches in the free world remember these injustices in their intercessions; too often they ignore the crises or simply remain ignorant that they are occurring.

The lack of emphasis on justice as a vital component of kingdom mission has in the past eroded the credibility of the church that remained at home in the West (i.e., those who did not go out on the mission field as missionaries). Large sections of the church at home in the West stood in silence as exploitation was carried out under colonialism, under racism, and under other oppressive and unjust campaigns by the nations of the West. This history now haunts those who carry the message of the kingdom of God in those nations that were the victims of oppression and exploitation by foreign forces.

We do not deny that a small minority of the church at home stood against such practices, but the larger church was blatantly silent and in fact participated in the spoils of such practices. While today colonialism is mostly history, the neocolonialism of economic power is an equally disturbing reality. The church cannot be silent when blatantly unjust economic and trade structures exploit the poor of the world.

We cannot be silent when the good life in one part of the world comes at the expense of the wanton exploitation of the environment in another area. There are terrible consequences for the people living there, consisting of loss of livelihood, displacement, massive environmental changes, famine, and death. In all of this we must ask, Where is the presence of Christ through his earthly representatives?

Too often we are not there. While many of us are unable to be there, on the scene, physically, we have the opportunity and responsibility to engage in one form or another from right where we are. And we have little excuse. In the modern media age, where news travels instantaneously via television, radio, print media, and the Internet, it is simply untenable for us to demur, "We just didn't know." We do not know only when we do not care to know.

"Christian" Human Rights?

The Universal Declaration of Human Rights is a comprehensive list of civil and political freedoms (often called "civil liberties") and various economic, social and cultural rights. It is a proclamation which the UN General Assembly approved on December 10, 1948. However, it is not a treaty that nations must ratify. Although many experts don't believe it has legal force, others argue that since it is used to interpret actions of various nations it has become part of customary law and is binding on all nations, whether or not they are members of the UN.

A Christian perspective on human rights is distinct from other approaches—though there is common ground. It is important to be clear about what distinguishes the varying perspectives, but also what values each individual approach shares with the others. The Universal Declaration of Human Rights, for instance, does not contradict Scripture. This statement affirms that the "inherent dignity of all members of the human family is the foundation of freedom, justice and peace in the world."

The declaration is universal, "a common standard of achievement for all peoples and all nations." Article 1 states that all "human beings are born free and equal in dignity and rights. They are endowed with reason and conscience and should act toward one another in a spirit of brotherhood." The rights to "life, liberty and security of a person"; equality before the law; freedom of movement; freedom of thought, conscience and religion; freedom of opinion and expression; and freedom of peaceful assembly and association are all biblical.

Indeed, it was Charles Malik, Lebanese ambassador, philosopher, and Christian, who insisted that the Universal Declaration include Article 18: The right to freedom of thought, conscience, and religion, including the right to change one's religious beliefs. He argued that unless the declaration "can create conditions which will allow man to develop ultimate loyalties . . . over and above his loyalty to the State, we shall have legislated not for man's freedom but for his virtual enslavement."[6]

Similarly, the prohibitions against slavery; torture; "cruel, inhuman or degrading treatment or punishment"; and arbitrary arrest, detention, or exile are consistent with Scripture. Christians might be particularly encouraged by Article 29, which states, as a counterweight to the language of rights, that everyone "has duties to the community in which alone the free and full development of his personality is possible." It goes on to say:

> In the exercise of his rights and freedoms, everyone shall be subject only to such limitations as are determined by law solely for the purpose of securing due recognition and respect for the rights and freedoms of

---

6. "Morality for Sale," Joe Loconte, *The New York Times*, April 1, 2004.

others and of meeting the just requirements of morality, public order and the general welfare in a democratic society.

Where there is common ground, Christians should be prepared to join forces with others who may not share our faith but who do share our compassion and our belief in human dignity and freedom. The Universal Declaration of Human Rights, along with accompanying established international laws, such as the International Covenant on Civil and Political Rights, can unite all who care about justice.

However, there are areas in which distinctively Christian human rights and more traditional human rights either diverge or in which a kingdom perspective adds a deeper level of understanding. Indeed, we would go further and state that a traditional conception of human rights—lacking any belief or root in God as the originator of these values—is dangerous.

Although it may start with the right intentions, a secular notion of human rights can lead to an erosion, rather than to the promotion, of right and wrong. "Unless we know what is the source of goodness and human dignity there will be no way of deciding what is good or bad for us," points out Howard Taylor in his book *Human Rights: Its Culture and Moral Confusions*.[7] He continues:

---

7. Howard Taylor, *Human Rights: Its Culture and Moral Confusions*, p. 3.

We will be lost in a sea of relativism where, inevitably, the strong will gain control over the weak and so destroy the very ideals that the concept of "human rights" was meant to protect and enhance. Unless the concept itself is grounded in a "morality which transcends the right," human rights will eventually deteriorate into human desires, and the concept will be powerless to protect the weak against the desires of the strong.

Os Guinness, in his book *Unspeakable*, argues that a Christian understanding of human rights is based on the *personal* nature of God: "He is personal because of his own nature, not because we need him to be personal," Guinness writes. He goes on to point out that God is not made in our image; we are made in his. There is no other ground for justifying the value and dignity of each human being. Those who strive for human rights without this understanding will quickly become disappointed.[8]

Responsibility:
At the Heart of Christian Human Rights

Gary Haugen, founder of the International Justice Mission, warns that the current generation of secular human rights

---

8. Os Guinness, *Unspeakable*, p. 146.

activists is in general being raised on a philosophy of "cultural relativism." Despite their best intentions, this means that "it is simply a matter of time before repression finds comfort in the moral vacuum." Without a "moral compass," the international human rights movement "may find it increasingly difficult to navigate its way . . . or to avoid being captured by the political fashion of the day."[9]

John Stott contends that Christians are called to provide that moral compass. The nature of human rights depends on the nature of the human beings whose rights they are. Thus, fundamental to human rights is the question of what it means to be human. Since the Bible focuses on the divine purpose for human beings, it has much to say on this topic. Three words seem to summarize its teachings—*dignity*, *equality,* and *responsibility*.[10] Stott reinforces this theme when he states:

> Here then is a Christian perspective on human rights. First, we affirm human dignity. Because human beings are created in God's image to know him, serve one another and be stewards of the earth, therefore they must be respected. Secondly, we affirm human equality. Because human beings have all been made in the same image by the same Creator, therefore we must not be obsequious

---

9. As quoted in *New Issues Facing Christians Today*, John Stott, p. 172.

10. Ibid., pp. 172–3.

to some and scornful to others, but behave without partiality to all. Thirdly, we affirm human responsibility. Because God has laid it upon us to love and serve our neighbours, therefore we must fight for their rights, while being ready to renounce our own in order to do so.[11]

Responsibility is at the heart of Christian human rights. A Christian is free to take a greater interest in his or her duty to protect the dignity and liberty of others than in his or her own rights.

Although we believe, as spelled out in the US Declaration of Independence, that human beings are born with certain inalienable rights, the very language of "rights" has arguably become so corroded by our modern "me"-focused society that we would do well to talk more in the biblical terms of justice, love, and righteousness.

Howard Taylor claims that there is a real danger that "rights" language corrupts the human relationships that are integral to the self-respect of a truly human life. Our humanity is found in the deeply personal relationships we have with one another. Our talk about "rights" tends to isolate us from one another and so diminish the very humanity it is supposed to protect.[12] Despite reservations about the terminology,

---

11. Ibid., p. 180.

12. Ibid., p. 7.

however, we will in this book use the terms *human rights* and *justice* interchangeably.

In His Image:
A Christian Understanding of Human Rights

A Christian understanding of human rights finds its inception in our basic belief in creation itself. God created human beings in his own image. In Genesis 1:26–27 we read: "Then God said, 'Let us make man in our image, in our likeness.' . . . So God created man in his own image, in the image of God he created him; male and female, he created them."

The Creator made every human being unique, but he at the same time created every one in his own image. All of life is prized by our Lord, and all people are of equal value from his perspective. In Acts 10:34 the apostle Peter remarks: "I now realize how true it is that God does not show favoritism but accepts men from every nation who fear him and do what is right."

Alfonso Wieland, director of a Peruvian human rights organization called Peace and Hope, asserts the following:

> It is essential that we understand that justice
> is not only God's concern, but is actually part
> of our own nature. All injustice is an assault
> on God and on his majesty and glory. As we

41

Christians call ourselves children of this God, we cannot fail to react when the dignity of a person is demeaned. This is not an option for us; it is an obligation that is central to our faith. We neglect the responsibility that comes along with being a child of God when we fail to pursue justice for our persecuted brothers and sisters. What does Jehovah ask of you? (Micah 6:8).[13]

What is involved in having been created in the image of God? It entails free will, equality with others, and individual dignity. One human being does not have the right to mar God's image placed in another person or to determine whether or not another individual should be allowed to live. On this basis murder, theft, and covetousness are wrong. The Ten Commandments provide the basic foundation for human rights, because many human rights violations are simply murder or theft by another name.

John Stott explains that we can summarize human dignity in these three ways: our relationship to God (or the right and responsibility of worship), our relationship to each other (or the right and responsibility of fellowship), and our relationship to the earth (or our right and responsibility of stewardship). He goes on to explain that all human rights involve the right to be human and to enjoy the dignity of having been created

---

13. Alfonso Wieland, *Tried by Fire*, pp. 13, 15.

in God's image and of having unique relationships to God, to one another, and to the material world.[14]

There is one further layer to the Christian understanding of human rights beyond creation, and that involves redemption and salvation. Our Creator has also redeemed and recreated us through the incarnation and atonement of his Son—at great personal cost. And the cost of God's redeeming work reinforces the sense of human worth his creation has already been given.[15]

Archbishop William Temple also contends that there can be no talk of "rights" except on the basis of faith in God. For if God is real, and all people are his sons and daughters, our worth comes as a result of that relationship. Our worth is what we are worth to God, and that is a great deal, for Christ died for us. At the same time, what gives each of us our highest worth imparts that same worth to everyone. In all that matters most we are all equal.[16]

But from a Christian perspective, "human rights" does not equate to libertarianism. John Stott argues that human rights are not unlimited rights, implying that we are free to be and do anything we want. They are limited to what is compatible with being the people God made us to be. Real freedom is

14. John Stott, *New Issues Facing Christians Today*, p. 174.

15. Ibid., p. 174.

16. As quoted by John Stott, *New Issues*, p. 174.

found only when we are being our true selves as authentic human persons, not when we contradict ourselves.[17]

Human Rights and the Unborn

If creation is the basis of human rights, and if human rights are limited to those rights that are compatible with "being human," then protection of the unborn is a clear concern for the Christian. We cannot justify the taking away of the life of the unborn child. The unborn child is in a most vulnerable position and challenges all our notions of human dignity, care, and responsibility. A low view of the girl child has resulted in gender-select abortions running close to two million per year in India. Female feticide has assumed alarming proportions and today threatens the very social balance of different communities in India. Some of these communities now buy young girls from other parts of India and indulge in the most blatant sexual trafficking. One abuse of human rights leads to another in a downward spiral of inhumanity.

The same right to life applies to all those who are physically or mentally challenged. Ending the life of such human beings is again a moral perversion reminiscent of the time when the Nazis first disposed of those Jews who had some physical aberration or infirmity.

---

17. Ibid., pp. 174–5.

Those who are sick, weak, and physically or mentally challenged are a gift to the human race because they call upon our deepest empathies, compassion, and humanity. As human beings they in turn contribute by giving us back our lost innocence, humility, and human bonding. No wonder Mother Teresa has stated that

> the life of the unborn child is a gift of God, the greatest gift God can make to the family. I am not discussing whether there is any need to legalise abortion or not. I simply believe that no human has the right to cut down a life. Every existence is the life of God in us. I feel the greatest destroyer of peace today is abortion, because it is a direct war, a direct killing, direct murder by the mother herself.[18]

Article 3 of the Universal Declaration of Human Rights protects "the right to life." Yet in the United Kingdom, since the Abortion Act of 1967, there have been six million abortions, a figure that translates into 600 abortions on every working day since the law's enactment. One in five pregnancies in that country ends in abortion. Lord Alton points out that because Britain has abandoned the sanctity of human life, the way has been paved for one million human embryos to be destroyed

---

18. Eileen Egan and Kathleen Egan, *Mother Teresa: Living the Word*, p. 79.

or experimented upon in the past ten years. "We create life, only to plunder it," he says. "We destroy life before birth with barely a thought, and now disabled people and the terminally ill are in our sights."[19]

In the United States, the statistics are even more sobering. A staggering 1.3 million babies are aborted each year—over 3,500 per working day, 150 per hour, 1 every 24 seconds. In the year 2000 alone, more babies in the US were killed through abortion than the sum total of Americans who died in the Revolutionary War, the Civil War; World Wars I and II, the wars in Korea, Vietnam, the Gulf, and Iraq combined. Since abortion laws were relaxed in the United States, there have been 40 million abortions, and 43 percent of women have undergone an abortion by the age of 45—meaning that every third child that is conceived is aborted.[20]

Where two "rights" collide, kingdom values demand that the right to life prevail. The fetus has a right to be born, and no human being is free to deny it that right. The right to life is the most fundamental of all human rights.

A stage further down the line are issues such as forced sterilization, as in China; child rape and forced marriage, as in Pakistan; mass infanticide, as in India; or—as in many countries—child labor, child prostitution, and human trafficking. How can the church keep quiet on these issues?

---

19. *The Tablet*, "Why we need a Norma," Lord Alton, March 20, 2004.

20. Jennifer O'Neill, "Women Deserve Better" campaign.

How can the state condone, indeed even enforce, such policies?

Human Rights and the Needs of Women

In Pakistan some estimate that between 70 and 90 percent of women experience domestic violence. Although child marriage is illegal, and the minimum age for marriage is eighteen, the law is continuously violated.

In southern Punjab, Muhammad Akmal was found guilty of sleeping with another man's wife, was fined 230,000 rupees ($4,000), and was ordered by the elders to marry off his two-year-old niece to Altaf Hussain, the forty-year-old husband of the woman he slept with, once she turned fourteen.[21]

In another village in southern Sindh, on May 4, 2005, a ten-year-old girl was forced to marry a fifty-year-old man. Her parents received a large sum of money for selling their daughter.[22]

Seven-year-old Sharee Komal, a Christian, was playing happily near her home in May, 2004, when she was lured away by an Islamic extremist. Found hours later near a graveyard under a railway bridge on the Qurban line, the little girl was hysterical, badly bruised, and covered in blood. She had

---

21. "Rough Justice of the Elders," *The Guardian Weekly*, May 20–26, 2005.

22. Ibid.

been brutally raped and tortured. "I thought she was dead," her mother reported five months later from a secret location. "The man tried to kill her by strangling her, and she was badly beaten around the head"—just because she was a Christian.

The treatment of women is an area in which the kingdom and the world differ in tone and emphasis, and sometimes in substance. And the church has often failed throughout the centuries to do its part to honor and protect women.

Although man was created first, and woman was formed from his rib, and although the apostle Paul teaches that women are to be submissive to their husbands, these Scripture passages have frequently been misconstrued to justify discrimination against women. For more than 2,000 years, half the population of the church has routinely been denied the opportunity to play their God-intended role.

Equality in Christian terms does not equate to sameness. Men and women are not identical. They have different characteristics, different bodies, and different kinds and levels of sensitivity. But women were created equal with men. He loves them equally, and they are to be accorded equal respect and dignity.

"We have equal rights because we have the same Creator," says John Stott. "Both the dignity and the equality of human beings are traced in Scripture to our creation. . . .

All human rights violations contradict the equality we enjoy by creation."[23]

The church has tolerated much deviant behavior by not fully grasping the teaching of equality that is available in the doctrine of creation. All human beings, both male and female persons, are equally formed in the image of God. Equality also means that regardless of race, color, caste, economics, or nationality, as human beings we are equal.

Racism, oppression, caste discrimination, and gender discrimination arise out of a faulty understanding of the overlying Christian principles that govern human social relations. Jesus was radical in his treatment of women, and at a time when men did not openly associate with women, Jesus dared to have women on his team. At a time when local prejudice was at its peak in connection to women doing "spiritual" or "religious" work, Jesus deployed them as evangelists/teachers when he sent the disciples out into the world.

As we look at church history, we must not forget that frequently the church has been a victim of the mores of the dominant cultures in which she has been placed. When these larger societies have allowed for racism, exploitation, and discrimination, the church also has participated in the social sins of the day.

---

23. John Stott, *New Issues Facing Christians Today*, p. 177.

The term *counter-cultural* has come to mean "exclusivity," keeping ourselves "holy" in the private life even as we participate both inside and outside the church in the blatant abuse of the equal rights of women and men. Exclusivity and self-righteousness were the blind spots of the religious leaders of Jesus' day. They lived in their own eyes such a life of exclusivity and self-righteousness that Jesus had to stipulate that in the eyes of God true religion is actually mercy, compassion, and justice.

If we are not just in our social behavior in the area of giving human beings their equality before God, then we are failing.

So who cares about the persecuted, the unborn, and women? And what does it matter if we do? In the next chapter we'll explore why we encounter so much injustice and learn how the church can respond to the desperate needs around the world.

Chapter Three

GOOD AND EVIL

The Reality

All we do know . . . is that evil labours with vast
power and perpetual success—in vain: preparing
always the soil for unexpected good to sprout in.

J. R. R. TOLKIEN—APRIL 1944

Jesus Christ understands injustice. After all, he has suffered
it himself. The world's most flagrant case of arbitrary arrest,
its most prominent instance of religious persecution, its most

brutal flogging, its most blatant travesty of justice, and the most infamous execution of an innocent man were all endured by Jesus Christ. It is hard to imagine, if you read the Gospel accounts or view *The Passion*, a more patent miscarriage of justice. Yet, despite it all, our Lord rose victorious.

We are in a very real sense engaged in a struggle between good and evil. You may not yet have realized this. If you are sitting comfortably in an armchair in your living room, with a can of soda or a bowl of ice cream, reading this book one evening after you have come home from work and put your children to bed, or returned from a church service where you sang heartwarming hymns about Jesus' love, you may not feel like you are in a struggle, but that is exactly what we all face today, and we need to be prepared.

The Bible clearly states that there is good and evil, justice and injustice in the world. The forces of good and evil work at the individual level, within the community, and in the wider society. Evil is quite capable of installing unjust structures in the world, instances in which the law itself is used to endorse injustice and destroy the weak, the poor, and the disenfranchised. This reality lies at the very heart of the Bible's message. In 1 Peter 5:8–9 Peter instructs his readers to

> be self-controlled and alert. Your enemy
> the devil prowls around like a roaring lion
> looking for someone to devour. Resist him,
> standing firm in the faith, because you know

that your brothers throughout the world are undergoing the same kind of sufferings.

In Romans 12:8, Paul cautions us that "love must be sincere" and urges us to "hate what is evil; cling to what is good." And in Mark 3:4 Jesus asks the Pharisees, after he has healed the man with a shriveled hand on the Sabbath: "Which is lawful on the Sabbath: to do good or to do evil, to save life or to kill?" In the Lord's Prayer (Matthew 6:9–10) we mouth the familiar words, "Our Father in heaven, hallowed be your name, your kingdom come, your will be done, on earth as it is in heaven." We also ask this God to "deliver us from the evil one" (v. 13).

Can there be any doubt about the prevalence of evil in this world? In Brazil alone between four and five adolescents are murdered daily, every twelve minutes a child is beaten, 4.5 million children under the age of twelve are working, 500,000 children are trapped in domestic labor, and 40 percent of crime victims are children. Is this not evil? On June 9, 2005, a twelve-year-old boy was discovered in a thicket in the neighborhood of Pirineu, in the city of Varzea Grande. He had been tortured and hanged, and his arms had been cut off. On May 9, 2005, a six-month-old girl was raped and killed, and on April 2 of the same year a three-year-old boy met the same fate.[1] No evil? When assassins roam freely and are willing to murder a child for as little as four dollars, when it is easier for

1. Lord Alton, "Street Children in Latin America," House of Lords Debate, Hansard, June 22, 2005, p. 1700.

a child to obtain a gun than a bus pass, and when children are routinely forced into prostitution, can we deny the power of evil?[2]

Evil schemes to displace God as the power behind the universe, and it does so through a concerted attack on divine order and harmony, on creation and humankind. It penetrates the heart of every person, and our choice, our struggle, is whether to respond by yielding to it or crushing it. It has several dimensions—personal, social, and structural.

Every individual faces temptations and struggles in the physical, sexual, financial, political, social, and spiritual realms. A society faces the challenge of how to treat its own members, as well as those in other societies. And social structures created by people can incorporate evil in the forms of injustice and oppression—sometimes subtly but in other cases blatantly and without challenge.

The conflict is between good and evil, between the kingdom of God and the realm of Satan. But what exactly is the kingdom of God?

In Mark 1:15—an account that takes place just after the unjust imprisonment of John the Baptist—Jesus goes to Galilee and proclaims, "The time has come. The kingdom of God is near. Repent and believe the good news!" That kingdom flows from the birth, life, teachings, arrest, flogging, crucifixion, death, and resurrection of Jesus Christ.

---

2. *The Streets Run Red with Blood*, Lord Alton, *Just Right*, Issue 10.

Many of our Lord's clearest messages about kingdom living were given in response to the stifling teachings and practices of the Pharisees. In Luke 17 he tells them: "The kingdom of God does not come with your careful observation, nor will people say, 'Here it is,' or 'There it is,' because the kingdom of God is within you."[3]

Later in the same passage, Jesus points out, "Whoever tries to keep his life will lose it, and whoever loses his life will preserve it."[4] In the very next chapter, Jesus instructs his disciples: "Let the little children come to me, and do not hinder them, for the kingdom of God belongs to such as these. I tell you the truth, anyone who will not receive the kingdom of God like a little child will never enter it."[5]

Perhaps the clearest explanation of the kingdom can be found in the Beatitudes, where Jesus says to his disciples:

> *God blesses those who are poor and realize their*
> *need for him,*
> *for the Kingdom of Heaven is theirs.*
> *God blesses those who mourn,*
> *for they will be comforted.*
> *God blesses those who are humble,*
> *for they will inherit the whole earth.*

---

3. Luke 17:20–21.

4. Luke 17:33.

5. Luke 18:16–17.

God blesses those who hunger and thirst for justice,
    for they will be satisfied.
God blesses those who are merciful,
    for they will be shown mercy.
God blesses those whose hearts are pure,
    for they will see God.
God blesses those who work for peace,
    for they will be called the children of God.
God blesses those who are persecuted for doing
    right,
    for the Kingdom of Heaven is theirs.[6]

In their book *The Lost Message of Jesus*, Steve Chalke and Alan Mann describe the kingdom as "the in-breaking *shalom* of God,"[7] available to us all. We often think of *shalom* as being synonymous with *peace*, but in fact the word, used many times throughout the Hebrew Scriptures, incorporates "contentment, health, justice, liberation, fulfilment, freedom and hope" and affects us in every aspect of life—"socially, economically, spiritually, and politically."[8]

---

6. Matthew 5:3–10 NLT.

7. Steve Chalke and Alan Mann, *The Lost Message of Jesus*, p. 16.

8. Ibid., p. 37.

Kingdom Mission: Both/And

Of what, then, does kingdom mission consist? For too long, the church has viewed its mission too narrowly. Leaders and followers in the church have adopted widely divergent perspectives, creating confusion for some and division for all. One segment of the church has regarded the preaching of the good news as its sole mission. Another part has contended that social action is the only valid gospel expression. Increasingly, evangelicals have begun to recognize that the Word preached *and* the Word expressed in social action are completely compatible, integral, and mutual.

Even so, many Christians view issues of human rights and justice differently from practical aid. While churches have increasingly embraced an involvement in helping the poor, the homeless, and the sick through outreaches to street sleepers at home or through donations to relief organizations such as World Vision or Tear Fund that are working abroad, the prospect of speaking out against injustice or lobbying for the rights of the oppressed unsettles them.

They view such activity as "political" action rather than as kingdom expressions of love. All too frequently Christians do not like to challenge the establishment, either because they are concerned about acting contentiously or because they view themselves as part of that establishment.

Yet Jesus was perpetually acting out on behalf of the oppressed. As Chalke and Mann argue, "At one and the same time Jesus' kingdom model enraged the establishment and delighted the ordinary citizens of Israel." These authors go on to point out that our Lord "had the audacity to declare that his alternative political, social, and religious manifesto was God's true agenda."[9] The real message of Jesus is found on every page of the Gospels. Jesus demonstrates love and redemption as he embraces the untouchable, feeds the hungry, eats with the socially and religiously unacceptable, forgives the unforgivable, heals the sick, and welcomes those on the margins to be his closest companions.[10]

Is there not an expression of human rights in Jesus' kingdom model?

Some evangelicals will continue to struggle. How do we express human rights as part of the kingdom without embracing the so-called "social gospel" or "liberation theology"? The answer is that we are called to provide an integrated message, starting with the central truth of Jesus' sacrifice for us on the cross, a vicarious punishment to pay the price for our sins. This is central to the struggle between good and evil. For Jesus' death and resurrection have two effects: individual and collective. He died to save each one of us from the otherwise tragic and inevitable results of our sins. But he also died to destroy evil.

---

9. Ibid., p. 24.

10. Ibid., p. 45.

In John 3:16–17 the Gospel writer declares,

> For God so loved *the world* that he gave his
> one and only Son, that whoever believes in
> him shall not perish but have eternal life. For
> God did not send his Son into *the world* to
> condemn the world, but to save the world
> through him (emphasis added).

In those two verses we find a clear expression of Jesus' sacrifice both for the individual—"whoever believes in him"—and the collective—"the world." Jesus' dying words were, "It is finished."[11] At that dramatic point the curtain of the temple was torn in two from top to bottom, the earth shook, and the rocks split.[12] God's Son died to destroy evil, not only in the spiritual realm but also in societal structures throughout history, for the two are inseparable.

By his death and resurrection, Jesus dealt with evil once and for all. No, it has not disappeared from the scene, but Christ has already attained the ultimate victory. For the time being, though, the struggle faced here on earth continues. Kingdom mission, then, is not only about my personal, eternal salvation; it is also about the defeat of evil and the ultimate, unchallenged rule of God over his redeemed creation.

---

11. John 19:30.

12. Matthew 27:51.

Kingdom mission is incomplete without the practice of justice and righteousness among the people of God and in the larger society. This is because kingdom mission is about facing sin and evil in this life, about setting right what is wrong, both in individual lives and in society at large. On both fronts, this happens only through the life-giving power of the Holy Spirit.

So-called kingdom mission that does not transform people and societies according to kingdom values results in what is commonly termed *Christianization*—an outward appearance of Christianity that in effect denies the power of the good news. Authentic kingdom mission invariably results in the Christ-transformation of our individual and social lives. It impacts how we live within our society and culture.

Christians who practice the both/and of *word and deed* do not subscribe to the world's distorted value system; rather, we are *in* the world but not *of* the world. The sheer excitement of the announcement of the kingdom in Jesus' teaching is uncovered in the emphasis upon that kingdom manifesting itself *here* and *now*. Indeed, it is already among us and in us! The kingdom, when functioning as it is intended, confronts evil and injustice and works vigorously to establish what is good and right in its place.

Eternal life is not just about eternal longevity. It is also about the quality of the God-life that is given to us here and now on the basis of the finished work of Jesus Christ. Mission is not only about making it to heaven; it is also about bringing heaven to a place on earth.

Kingdom Mission: All of the Above

Kingdom mission, properly understood, involves several components working together for the sake of the gospel—not one at the expense of another, but all in tandem, manifesting the Christian message to the world. The core components are *proclamation, service, community, justice,* and *reclamation.*

Proclamation—*kerygma* in Greek—communicating the good news of the gospel through words, is essential, and it is an area in which Christians have historically been focused.

Service, or *diakonia,* on the other hand, involves practical, tangible expressions of compassion—going to a place of poverty, suffering, or devastation; providing food, medicines, education, construction, expertise, and training; reaching out to show God's love. This could be as simple as visiting an elderly woman in your neighborhood on a regular basis, doing her shopping, and cooking her meals, or as complex as going overseas to minister to people who are being persecuted or suffering from poverty, famine, earthquake, floods, disease, or conflict.

Community, or *koinonia,* has to do with the creation of new groupings and fellowships. This entails not simply planting new churches, although that is an important component, but also fighting to preserve, and in places revive, communities that are systematically being destroyed by the secular state—sometimes at the most basic level, the family unit.

Justice, or *dikaiosune*, involves sharing in Jesus' mission as set out in Luke 4:16–21, when our Lord quoted the ringing words of Isaiah 61:1–2: "The Spirit of the Lord . . . has sent me to proclaim freedom for the prisoners and recovery of sight for the blind, to release the oppressed."

When Jesus lay down the scroll following this reading, he informed the astonished gathering in the synagogue that "today this scripture is fulfilled in your hearing" (Luke 4:21).

Missiologist Charles R. Taber contends that *justice* is at the heart of the kingdom:

> Building on, but radically extending, hints found in Hebrew Law and Prophets, Jesus alone among all religious founders and leaders rejected all forms of discrimination and insisted that all human beings ought to be treated in exactly the same way. His own dealings with women, with children, with lepers and other ritually polluted people, and with foreigners, radically undermined all the distinctions that human society of his day institutionalized. He extended the category "neighbor" to *all humankind* and insisted that the two Great Commandments applied to all. These surely were the reasons why Jesus'

peers found him troublingly subversive and therefore condemned him.[13]

Kingdom mission also involves *krisis*, the work of discerning what is evil and what is good, and acting on behalf of what is determined to be good. And it involves *reclamation* or stewardship of all of God's creation—including the environment and animal life. Why have we left it to the environmental extremists to decry pollution and promote environmental protection? Christians should be the ultimate "green" activists, defending God's creation while refraining from the worship of creation itself.

The church has generally upheld a laudable record of "service"—the provision of medical or educational services to the poor, the establishment and maintenance of orphanages, caring for the homeless, and the distribution of humanitarian aid to disaster areas are all examples. These highly significant, tangible actions may be defined as "social service," or, as John Stott puts it, "relieving human need." But these are not the only effective expressions of Christian social concern.

Stott acknowledges that it is "always good to feed the hungry." But the church must not neglect the twin sister of social service, namely social action—"removing the causes of human need; seeking to transform the structures of society; the quest for justice." As Stott adds, while feeding the hungry is

13. Charles R. Taber, International Bulletin of Missionary Research, June 2002.

good, "it is better if possible to eradicate the causes of hunger. So if we truly love our neighbours and want to serve them, our service may oblige us to take (or solicit) political action on their behalf." Social action and social service go together—so much so that "it would be very artificial to divorce them."[14]

If we combine all five of these components in our strategies and experience (*proclamation, service, community, justice,* and *reclamation*), and we have a clear personal relationship with Jesus Christ, founded on prayer and a commitment to the truth of the Scriptures, we are living out biblical kingdom values, not a "social gospel" focused exclusively on human rights. If we act out of a genuine response to the free gift of grace given to us by God, not out of a belief that we need to earn our salvation, we are truly reflecting the kingdom mission. Our good deeds do not gain us salvation, but if we are saved, we will naturally desire to live as Jesus has taught us.

Corrie ten Boom in *The Hiding Place* describes watching her aunt die, secure in the knowledge that no good deeds she had done could ever have won her a place in heaven:

> As we listened in disbelief, she lowered her hands and with tears coursing down her face whispered: "Dear Jesus, I thank you that we must come with empty hands. I thank you that you have done all—all—on the Cross,

---

14. John Stott, *New Issues Facing Christians Today*, p. 15.

and that all we need in life or death is to be
sure of this."[15]

Corrie ten Boom's family saved the lives of many Jews
by providing them a place of sanctuary—but they did this
because Jesus was already at work in their lives, not in order
to win his favor.

Our Christian work becomes a "social gospel" only if
we deny the first three elements—proclamation, service, and
community—and instead pursue justice for the sake of justice,
as an end in itself. If we have no reference to personal faith in
Christ, and justice becomes the sole "cause" we pursue, we are
no longer engaged in kingdom mission. But if the reference
point is personal faith in Christ, each one of us needs to be
involved, in some way, in all five elements; otherwise, we are
not being faithful to Christ.

The biblical writer James makes this abundantly clear:

> What good is it, my brothers, if a man claims
> to have faith but has no deeds? Can such
> faith save him? Suppose a brother or sister is
> without clothes and daily food. If one of you
> says to him, "Go, I wish you well; keep warm
> and well fed," but does nothing about his
> physical needs, what good is it? In the same
> way, faith by itself, if it is not accompanied

---

15. Corrie Ten Boom, *The Hiding Place*, p. 39.

by action, is dead. . . . As the body without the spirit is dead, so faith without deeds is dead.[16]

Our Christian work becomes lopsided evangelism, however, when we deny the last two elements—justice and reclamation—by proclaiming the good news of the gospel and nothing more. Peter Kuzmic, founding director of the Evangelical Theological Faculty in Osiejk, Croatia, concludes that proclamation of the gospel alone, especially in areas of conflict, disaster, and suffering, is unbiblical and counterproductive.

It smacks of religious propaganda and senseless proselytizing. People do not only have souls that we register for heaven; they also have bodies that need to be taken care of. They have not only ears to hear what we say; they also have eyes to observe whether we truly live according to what we proclaim. There is no authentic mission without the motivation of love and the practice of compassion.

Read that far, and we might still be comfortably nodding in agreement while looking to others to act. But Kuzmic

---

16. James 2:14–17, 26.

concludes: "Indifference to suffering and injustice is a sin."[17] John Stott adds that "too many of us evangelicals either have been, or maybe still are, irresponsible escapists." He continues:

> Fellowship with each other in the church is much more congenial than service in an apathetic and even hostile environment outside. . . . Instead of seeking to evade our social responsibility, we need to open our ears and listen to the voice of him who calls his people in every age to go out into the lost and lonely world (as he did), in order to live and love, to witness and serve, like him and for him. For that is "mission." Mission is our human response to the divine commission.[18]

Kingdom Mission: A Consensus

The integration of these different aspects of mission has been part of a long process in landmark conferences and declarations. In 1966, at a US mission conference, delegates unanimously supported what became known as the Wheaton Declaration, which clearly links "a verbal witness to Jesus

---

17. Peter Kuzmic, *Justice, Mercy, and Humility,* p. 158.

18. John Stott, *New Issues Facing Christians Today*, p. 18.

Christ" and "evangelical social action." In addition, the document urges "all evangelicals to stand openly and firmly for social equality, human freedom, and all forms of social justice throughout the world."[19]

This was followed by the International Congress on World Evangelization in Lausanne, Switzerland, in July 1974. This landmark conference brought together 2,700 evangelicals from 150 nations under the theme "Let the Earth Hear His Voice."[20] The resulting Lausanne Covenant declared:

> We affirm that God is both the Creator and Judge of all men. We therefore should share his concern for justice and reconciliation throughout human society and for the liberation of men from every kind of oppression. Because mankind is made in the image of God, every person, regardless of race, religion, colour, culture, class, sex or age, has an intrinsic dignity because of which he should be respected and served, not exploited. Here too we express penitence both for our neglect and for having sometimes regarded evangelism and social concern as mutually exclusive. Although reconciliation with man is not reconciliation with God, nor

---

19. As quoted in *New Issues Facing Christians Today*, John Stott, p. 11.

20. Ibid., p. 12.

is social action evangelism, nor is political liberation salvation, nevertheless we affirm that evangelism and socio-political involvement are both part of our Christian duty. For both are expressions of our doctrines of God and man, our love for our neighbour and our obedience to Jesus Christ. The message of salvation implies also a message of judgment upon every form of alienation, oppression and discrimination, and we should not be afraid to denounce evil and injustice wherever they exist. When people receive Christ they are born again into his kingdom and must seek not only to exhibit but also to spread its righteousness in the midst of an unrighteous world. The salvation we claim should be transforming us in the totality of our personal and social responsibilities. Faith without works is dead.

This statement was supported by churches worldwide in 1974—but it has not yet been fully practiced.[21]

This proclamation has been further endorsed by gatherings such as the International Consultation on Gospel and Culture in Willowbank, Bermuda, in 1978; the All India Conference on Evangelical Social Action in Madras in 1979; the Second Latin

---

21. As quoted in *Out of the Comfort Zone*, George Verwer, p. 135.

American Congress on Evangelism in Lima, Peru, in 1979; the International Consultation on Simple Lifestyle in 1980; the Consultation on the Relationship Between Evangelism and Social Responsibility in Grand Rapids, Michigan, in 1982; the National Association of Evangelicals in Bournemouth, UK, in 1996; and at various other international gatherings. But while the wording is laudable, where is the transforming action on the part of every Christian in the free and wealthy world?

John Stott endorses the views outlined at Wheaton and Lausanne but cautions against "political correctness" that waters down the gospel and leads to a politicized theology. "We should set ourselves in Christ's name against all dehumanising tendencies, against anything and everything that impedes human freedom and fulfilment," he writes in *The Incomparable Christ.*[22] It is important to note the phrase "in Christ's name." Liberation is a legitimate goal, but to what end? Not simply for our own desires, Stott argues, but for God's purposes:

> We need to redefine liberation. It is intended to secure our freedom from anything and everything that inhibits human beings from being what God by creation and redemption intends them to be.

22. John Stott, *The Incomparable Christ,* p. 115.

Integral mission has perhaps been best expressed by the organizers of the Micah Network,[23] a group of 140 Christian leaders, theologians, and practitioners from 50 countries, who met in Oxford in 2001. In a book titled *Justice, Mercy and Humility: Integral Mission and the Poor,* they define integral mission, or holistic transformation, as

the proclamation and demonstration of the Gospel. It is not simply that evangelism and social involvement are to be done alongside each other. Rather, in our integral mission our proclamation has social consequences as we call people to love and repentance in all areas of life. And our social involvement has evangelistic consequences as we bear witness to the transforming grace of Jesus Christ.

If we ignore the world, we betray the word of God which sends us out to serve the world. If we ignore the word of God, we have nothing to bring to the world. Justice and justification by faith, worship and political action, the spiritual and the material, personal change and structural change, belong together. As in the life of Jesus, being, doing and saying are at the heart of our integral task.[24]

---

23. See *www.micahnetwork.org.*

24. Tim Chester (Editor), *Justice, Mercy and Humility*, p. 19.

Kingdom Mission: In the Beginning

One of the first human rights activists in human history was Moses. Just after God had revealed himself to his chosen servant in the burning bush, he informed him:

> I have indeed seen the misery of my people in Egypt. I have heard them crying out because of their slave drivers, and I am concerned about their suffering. So I have come down to rescue them from the hand of the Egyptians. . . . And now the cry of the Israelites has reached me, and I have seen the way the Egyptians are oppressing them.[25]

It is noteworthy that God declined to intervene directly to stop the oppression of his people. He could easily have done so. He most certainly did not need to depend on people to do it for him. But he chose to use Moses.

And he works in the same way today. He could intervene directly, in all his majesty, in Sudan, Burma, North Korea, Cuba, and elsewhere, but instead he instructs us, as he once did Moses, "So now, go. I am sending you to Pharaoh to bring my people the Israelites out of Egypt."[26]

---

25. Exodus 3:7–9.

26. Exodus 3:10.

Will we respond in the affirmative? Or will we respond like Moses did, under the influence of his fallible human nature: "Who am I, that I should go to Pharaoh and bring the Israelites out of Egypt?"[27] Will we protest further by echoing Moses' objection, "O Lord, I have never been eloquent, neither in the past nor since you have spoken to your servant. I am slow of speech and tongue"[28]? Will we try to wash our hands of the whole issue, by entreating with Moses, "O Lord, please send someone else to do it."[29] That is precisely how many in the church have responded to God's clear call to us ever since Moses' time to challenge the pharaohs of this world.

Many of the Old Testament prophets followed Moses in his ultimate obedience by serving as a voice for the voiceless. The prophets were courageous in denouncing tyrants, especially the kings of Israel and Judah. Just because they were monarchs, and even "the Lord's anointed," they were not above criticism and rebuke.[30]

But we do not face this struggle alone or in our own strength. We rely on a God who equips us with all we need: "Who gave man his mouth? Who makes him deaf or mute? Who gives him sight or makes him blind? Is it not I, the Lord?

27. Exodus 3:11.

28. Exodus 4:10.

29. Exodus 4:13.

30. John Stott, *New Issues Facing Christians Today*, p. 177.

Now go; I will help you speak and will teach you what to say."[31]

This struggle against evil involves taking risks, stepping out of our comfort zones, even putting our lives on the line. John Eldredge argues that much of the church has forgotten this: "We have settled for safety in numbers—a comfortable, anonymous distance," he contends.[32] This behavior is in stark contrast to Jesus' teaching that "greater love has no man than this, that he lay down his life for his friends."[33]

Dietrich Bonhoeffer, in his *Letters and Papers from Prison*, argues that we need to heed Jesus' radical example:

> Our capacity to sympathise with others in their sufferings is strictly limited. We are not Christs, but if we want to be Christians we must show something of Christ's breadth of sympathy by acting responsibly, by grasping our "hour," by facing danger like free men, by displaying a real sympathy which springs not from fear, but from the liberating and redeeming love of Christ for all who suffer. To look on without lifting a hand is most un-Christian.[34]

31. Exodus 4:11–12.

32. John Eldredge, *Waking the Dead*, p. 198.

33. John 15:12–15.

34. Dietrich Bonhoeffer, *Letters and Papers from Prison*, p. 145.

Kingdom Mission: What Makes the Difference?

How we go about confronting evil is key, however, and in the field of human rights it is our methodology that distinguishes a Christian approach. The apostle Peter directs his readers to be "sympathetic, love as brothers, be compassionate and humble. Do not repay evil with evil or insult with insult, but with blessing, because to this you were called so that you may inherit a blessing."[35]

We are called to "turn from evil and do good," to "seek peace and pursue it."[36] In Romans 12:19, Paul teaches us not to seek revenge, pointing out that vengeance is within God's jurisdiction. On the contrary, in Jesus' own words, "if your enemy is hungry, feed him; if he is thirsty, give him something to drink."[37]

This may sound contradictory. We talk of a united strategy to confront evil, but then we express our need to offer blessing and sympathy and humility, to feed our enemies! The key to this paradox may be found in Romans 12:21: "Do not be overcome by evil, but overcome evil with good." We are most definitely to fight evil—including injustice—with all the fierceness, energy, dedication, commitment, sacrifice, and courage we can muster, but we are to fight and overcome it *with good*. In short, we are called to be fierce in doing good.

---

35. 1 Peter 3:8–9.

36. 1 Peter 3:11.

37. Romans 12:20.

In a small town called Los Palos, at the eastern end of the half-island of East Timor, lies a convent. The nuns there are Indonesian, but they have stayed in East Timor since the small island nation gained its tumultuous independence. In 1999, during the violence following its referendum, while the Indonesian military and militia were slaughtering thousands, looting and destroying, these Indonesian nuns stayed on in Los Palos to help the wounded.

One day an Indonesian soldier came to the door of the convent and knocked. A sister opened the door, and the soldier ordered her and all the other nuns into a truck to depart for Indonesia. The nuns refused, affirming that their place was in East Timor with the suffering and wounded. Aghast at having his orders disobeyed so blatantly, the soldier asked the nun: "Don't you know who I am? I am military." The nun smiled gently, but stood firm in her task. The soldiers departed, and the nuns continued to treat the wounded. They had no apparent power at their disposal; yet, empowered by the Lord, they overcame evil with good.

There are two fatal errors we as Christians can make in response to evil. We can claim that evil and sin are simply confined to the sphere of personal morality. Or we can adopt a passive attitude that lacks any impetus or theology to actively combat evil and its roots.

The battle between good and evil continues to rage. More soldiers and civilians have been killed in wars in the twentieth century than in the previous 5,000 years of recorded history combined, and four times as many as in the previous four centuries, cumulatively. Over 112 million people were killed in the century that is just behind us, a century Solzhenitsyn described as the most cannibalistic in all of human history.[38] Still today, at least 1 million children are forced into prostitution each year, and in India alone there are 15 million children in bonded slavery.[39]

But the day will come when all of this will end. As Paul asserts in 1 Corinthians 15:24, "The end will come, when [Christ] hands over the kingdom to God the Father after he has destroyed all dominion, authority and power." We can be confident that "death has been swallowed up in victory," a victory God gives us "through our Lord Jesus Christ."[40] Yes, we have the victory, but there is still work to be done. Each of us is to "give [our]selves fully to the work of the Lord, because [we] know that [our] labor in the Lord is not in vain."[41] The slumbering giant, Christ's church, is slowly beginning to wake up to the work all around and the work ahead—until our final victory is sealed.

A Christian worker living along the Thai-Burmese border, providing relief to refugees from Burma in the camps in Thailand and to internally displaced people inside Burma, penned both the following prayer and the call to prayer, an appropriate way to end this chapter before going on to consider

---

38. Peter Kuzmic, *Justice, Mercy & Humility*, p. 151.

39. Ibid., p. 193.

40. 1 Corinthians 15:54, 57.

41. 1 Corinthians 15:58.

in greater depth what actions we might take—as kingdom people—to halt human rights violations around the world. Join us in making these ours today, and every day:

> The refugee drama is played out on a daily basis with reports of suffering I cannot even imagine. The pictures make me sick. The news is like the ocean's force; one wave followed by another with seemingly endless bad news and erosion in a country rich in natural resources and full of beautiful people.

> More than anything, my prayer tonight is for those souls that live in fear for their lives, for the new mothers and old fathers, for the children making toys of bamboo and stones, for all those millions of innocent people living on the wrong end of a machine gun. God, may your kingdom come and your will be done on earth as it is in heaven tonight. For the refugees and their God. Amen

Tonight before you go to bed, please remember to whisper a prayer on behalf of the orphaned children, the molested women, and the men who just want to go home and work in their rice fields by day and play with their kids as the sun sets. Pray that they would blow the candle out on another day, remembering not just the bitterness of their loss, but the goodness of God and his grace. Pray that all of us who serve them would be used to that end—to share the love and grace we have been given by Jesus himself.

Chapter Four

SALT AND LIGHT

The Response

Concepts such as truth, justice and compassion
cannot be dismissed as trite when these are often the
only bulwarks which stand against ruthless power.

AUNG SAN SUU KYI

Standing beneath the shade of a tamarind tree in his
native Sudan, celebrating Sunday services with his people, the
exiled bishop, Macram Gassis, smuggled by an international

Christian human rights group into southern Sudan, spoke these words:

> This most beautiful cathedral, not built with human hands, but by nature and by God, is filled with the people of God. We must tell our brothers and sisters that the people here are still full of hope and that they still smile, in spite of suffering and persecution. Your people have suffered slavery, but you are not slaves to the world but children of God, who has told us we can call him "Abba, Father."

> Christianity gives us liberty; therefore we are no longer slaves, but free: children of liberty, freedom and truth. But we live in a bad world. Many of your people have been sold into slavery. But that is not to become a slave . . . the real slave is a slave to sin; who does injustice to brothers and sisters; who kills them. Some people feel naked because they have no clothes and they try to cover themselves because of their embarrassment. But this is not real nakedness. True nakedness is to be without love. Therefore be clothed in love. This is Christianity.[1]

---

1. Baroness Cox.

With Liberty and Justice *for All?*

Those words capture the essence of this book: that kingdom mission requires justice. For justice is love, and Christ's followers are to love in his name. A Christian understanding of human rights, reduced to its basics, is focused on obedience to the command to love the Lord our God with everything we have and to love our neighbors as much as we love ourselves.

Many Christians are unprepared to get their hands dirty in the promotion of human rights—the practical dimension of loving others in his name. They walk away from the issues, shield their eyes, wash their hands—and in so doing, they are, perhaps inadvertently, complicit with the oppressors.

Others are willing to engage with issues of justice, but only when that injustice affects fellow Christians. Or worse, only certain types of Christians. An evangelical, for example, might be up in arms about the arrest of a fellow evangelical pastor or Christian worker in Vietnam or Iran—but would he cry out when a Catholic church is attacked? The idea that we should speak up for people of other denominations, or other faiths, or for those of no faith, is disturbing to some. Yet fighting exclusively for one's own kind reveals a grotesquely shortsighted and limited vision of the kingdom.

While we do indeed have a special responsibility to speak up for our persecuted brothers and sisters in Christ, we must also speak up for all other downtrodden human beings, regardless of creed, because all have been created in the image of God.

Speaking on behalf of the persecuted church is an essential component of a Christian approach to human rights. If we do not advocate for our brothers and sisters in Christ who are suffering, who will? In 1 Corinthians 12:26 we are told, with reference to the body of Christ, that "if one part suffers, every part suffers with it." And in Galatians 6:10 Paul instructs his fellow believers, "As we have opportunity, let us do good to all people, especially to those who belong to the family of believers."

Just as we would in our own blood families, so in our spiritual family, the body of Christ, we are to speak up for our brothers and sisters who are being persecuted. So, when a hundred Protestant house-church Christians are arrested in Henan Province, China, as they were on August 6, 2004, following a raid on their retreat site by more than two hundred police and military personnel, we have a responsibility to protest. When eight underground Roman Catholic priests and two seminarians are arrested in Hebei Province, China, we need to intervene. When four Christians are arrested in Vientiane, Laos, and a house church there is closed down, as happened in August 2004, we are to protest to the authorities in that country as well as in our own.

When a young Indonesian Christian stands firm in his faith in the face of an Islamist jihad warrior, whose response is to chop off the boy's arms with a machete and eviscerate him, we are obliged to cry out. When churches are attacked in

Sri Lanka and Buddhist parliamentarians propose legislation to criminalize religious conversions, it is our duty to campaign against this outrage. When a Christian such as Javed Anjum is tortured to death by Islamists in Pakistan, or Samuel Masih is killed by a policeman who attacks him with a brick cutter, we are failing in our biblical responsibility to help the family of believers if we remain silent.

When three churches, a school, a convent, and many Christian homes are attacked and burned down in a place like Sangla Hill, Pakistan, as happened in November 2005, we are under obligation to speak out against such violence. When nine Christian converts, mainly women and girls, in Orissa, India, are seized, stripped, paraded through the village, beaten, and then tortured by Hindu extremists because they will not renounce their Christian faith, we are neglecting the interests of our own faith, which is under enemy fire, if we fail to stand in solidarity with our persecuted sisters and brothers.

Speaking up for our own family is the starting point. But we cannot end there. When Buddhists or Muslims or Falun Gong practitioners are persecuted, we must not stay silent. We may disagree with their theology, but we must, if we are true to the gospel, vigorously defend their right to believe and practice their faith—or live without faith of any kind—so long as they do not infringe on others' rights to freedom of conscience. Speaking out for the rights of others is perhaps the most powerful form of witness for the gospel. It is also a matter of self-interest, for persecuted Christians are more likely to gain help from people of different faiths if they themselves have stood in the gap for others.

In 2002 thousands of Muslims in Gujarat, India, were massacred. There was rioting in the streets, mass rape, devastation, and carnage, all created by Hindu fundamentalists. Who stepped in to help these hapless victims? Along with a few other groups, the All India Christian Council, at considerable risk to its personnel, set up camps in Gujarat and provided shelter and food for the vulnerable, displaced Muslims for six weeks. This was a statement of enormous courage, love, and commitment.

Furthermore, these Christians did not publicize their act of love to the outside world, nor did they attempt to convert anyone. Taking their cue from Jesus' teaching in Matthew 6:1–5, which urges us to be careful not to do our "acts of righteousness" in front of others, they simply got down to work treating the injured, housing the homeless, feeding the hungry, and clothing the naked. Subsequently, however, the news spread, and the Muslim community throughout India opened its arms to Christians as never before.

Across the nation, All India Christian Council leaders received invitations to speak to large audiences of Muslims— sometimes as many as 75,000 people—and invariably the topic they were invited to address was: "Why did you help us? What does the Bible have to say about human rights and justice?" Their hearts were warmed and open as never before.

The All India Christian Council has also developed pioneering solidarity with the Dalit community, the 250 million so-called "untouchables" and "scheduled tribes" or "outcastes" in India who for more than three thousand years have been oppressed, standing as they do on the bottom rung of India's caste hierarchy.

When five Dalits were lynched for skinning a dead cow, Udit Raj, a Dalit leader, turned to the All India Christian Council for solidarity. Indian Christian leaders traveled to New Delhi within hours of the tragedy. There they joined a protest and met with the parents of the victims. They provided the families with humanitarian assistance and comforted them in their grief. The statement the Christians were making was that these Dalits were human beings and that it was the caste system that consigned them to work with animals—a statement in direct contrast to that of a Hindu nationalist leader, who asserted that a cow is more valuable than a Dalit.

On November 4, 2001, approximately 100,000 Dalits gathered for a mass conversion rally. Tens of thousands more were stopped from reaching the assembly by the police and by Hindu extremists. Trains were unnecessarily delayed, buses were pulled off roads, and people were threatened. The two Hindu extremist groups, the Vishwa Hindu Parishad (VHP) and the Rastriya Swam Sevak Sangh (RSS), claimed that the whole event was a Christian conspiracy. To make matters worse, some Christians were accused by the extremists of seeking to make personal financial gain in the name of "Christian conversions." Despite this bad press, the event sparked a major movement of Dalits across the nation rejecting Hinduism.

Ram Raj, who became Udit Raj upon his conversion from Hinduism to Buddhism, urged Dalits to "quit Hinduism" and embrace any other religion that could draw them out of oppression and give them freedom of choice and conscience, as well as personal dignity. He thanked the Indian Christian community for its solidarity with the Dalits and invited three Christian leaders to speak from the platform. These leaders delivered a simple message—that they stood in solidarity with the oppressed, that they loved the Dalit people, and that Jesus Christ loved the Dalit people.

The Dalits who converted were making both a social statement and a religious one, yet theirs was also a choice for a just system. "The conversion is a rejection of whatever caste stands for. It is a great walkout from Hinduism," Udit Raj informed the crowds. The majority chose Buddhism. But what is interesting (and to some Christians incomprehensible) is that the All India Christian Council stood with these Dalits, whatever religion they chose. It was a stirring witness on the part of the Christians to let the Dalits know that they are loved by Jesus Christ and his followers and that Christians would support their right to be free even when they opted for Buddhism over Christianity.

What would the implicit message have been had the Christians chosen the alternative: to walk away, disassociate from the Dalits, and refuse to love them unless they converted to Christianity? Christ's love for us is, after all, unconditional.

He presents himself to us, as he presents himself to the Dalits through his church in India today, and he offers us a choice— an invitation. He says in Revelation 3:20: "Here I am! I stand at the door and knock. If anyone hears my voice and opens the door, I will go in and eat with him, and he with me."

This is supported in Revelation 22:17: "The Spirit and the bride say 'Come!' And let him who hears say 'Come!' Whoever is thirsty, . . . let him take the free gift of the water of life." Our Lord does not force himself upon us, nor does he break down the door of our hearts. Like a gentleman he knocks and offers us a gift, free for the taking.[2]

In a further act of solidarity with the Indian Dalit community, in March 2004, the All India Christian Council hosted a two-day human rights conference in Hyderabad. The first day saw a gathering of a thousand Indian Christian leaders dedicated to Christian human rights and religious freedom. It was a call to arms—not militarily, but spiritually and socially—a wake-up call for the church in India to the cause of justice. The theme of the conference was "Standing Together in the Face of Persecution," and it addressed a problem that had dogged India for much of the previous decade: the rise of militant Hinduism and the persecution of Christians.

---

2. Indian Christian solidarity with the Dalits was not simply a one-off act. The All India Christian Council has continued to make the Dalit freedom struggle their focus. The Dalit Freedom Network (www.dalitnetwork.org) was formed in 2003 to assist the Dalits in the areas of education, social justice, economic development, and healthcare.

Ever since Bibles had been burned in Rajkot by the Bajrang Dal in 1998, and a group of nuns had been raped there, the situation had deteriorated. The Australian missionary Graham Staines and his sons Timothy, nine, and Phillip, seven, were burned alive as they slept in their car in 1999. The telling response from then Prime Minister Atal Behari Vajpayee (a member of the Sangh Parivar and a Hindu nationalist himself) was a call for a national debate on conversions. Several Indian states introduced anti-conversion laws, and hate literature was distributed in various communities.

Yet despite the fact that the Christian community had enormous problems of its own to deal with, the focus of the conference was not inward. Instead, in addition to discussing the persecution they themselves faced, the Christian organizers of the conference included on their agenda the Dalit struggle, and Udit Raj was a keynote speaker.

The second day of the conference was markedly different from the first, but no less spiritually enriching. This was an interfaith gathering, attended by Christians, Muslims, Buddhists, Sikhs, moderate Hindus, and Dalits, all of whom in one way or another had become the targets of the extremist Hindus. There were Indian, British, American, Australian, and Norwegian participants. And, most symbolically, the conference ended that day with a lunch, in a large marquee, at which the delegates sat cross-legged on the floor at low tables with large plates of curry and rice, eating the food with their fingers from the same plate as their neighbors.

A Muslim, a Christian, a Hindu, a Buddhist, and a Dalit sat together eating from the same plate. An Indian and a Westerner sat as equals, sharing from a mutual plate. People who would never have considered eating together under ordinary circumstances, and who most certainly would not have shared a communal plate, sat side-by-side for an hour or so in perfect harmony and without embarrassment. Recalling the occasion, it seems obvious that this is precisely what Jesus had in mind when he declared that peacemakers are blessed and will be called sons of God (Matthew 5:9).

One for All, and All for One

It is not difficult to imagine some Christian readers feeling acutely uncomfortable with the events described above, if indeed they have stayed with us this far. So we must raise an attempt to respond to a vital question at this stage: How can we avoid falling into syncretism when faced with mutual challenges addressed by members of different religions? The answer is as uncomplicated as the distinction: Syncretism (the fusion or combination of different belief systems) results only when we compromise the basic fundamentals of the Christian faith and the uniqueness of Jesus Christ.

That is not at all what we are arguing for here. While our sense of kingdom mission requires us not to compromise our core beliefs—the divinity of Jesus Christ; his birth, death, and resurrection for the salvation of humankind; the power of the Holy Spirit; the creation of the world by God the Father—

it also requires us to avoid the other extreme: isolationism, exclusion, and judgmentalism.

Jesus teaches us clearly that we are to love *our neighbor* as ourselves (Matthew 19:19). Scripture does not direct us simply to love our *Christian* neighbor, to speak up only for the *Christian* oppressed, to offer help exclusively to the *Christian* sick and hungry and imprisoned. If we are true to the gospel imperative and Jesus' own example, we will avoid the extremes of either syncretism or exclusivity.

On that basis, we as Christ's followers do well to continuously look for areas where we can connect with the non-Christian world. We can communicate the gospel through cooperation with others in areas of common interest much more effectively than when we stand outside of society and harang passersby with condemnation and criticism.

Although there are critical areas of theology in which we as Christians differ from those of other faiths, we can still connect with Muslims, Jews, Buddhists, and Hindus on many moral issues. In terms of religious freedom, in some countries one religion is dominant and seeks to oppress the others. But in pluralistic societies such as India or the Western democracies, moderates from each faith group can work together to combat both fundamentalism and secularization.

So, if the state is attempting to remove religion from the education system, religious groups can unite in opposition. To defend Christian children from being deprived of their heritage, we can collaborate with those of other faiths to campaign for prayer, according to the person's individual faith choice, to be restored to the education system.

Modern Christianity has been much more compromising in the face of secularization than have other faiths. We as Christians have much to learn in this area from those espousing other major belief systems. We do well to follow their lead in developing the moral fiber many of them continue to assert.

The growing HIV/AIDS crisis in the developing world is another area of potential cooperation for those of different faiths. Indeed, in India the idea has been promoted that the leaders of all the major religions should work together to campaign against HIV/AIDS: to unite around the belief that sexual intercourse is to be practiced exclusively within the marriage bond and that both premarital sex and infidelity are wrong.

Religious leaders could even unite in the face of fundamentalism. The rise of militant Islam is not only a danger to Christians, Jews, and the West, but also to moderate Muslims. Indeed, it is Muslims who suffer most from the introduction of Islamic or "Sharia" laws. Similarly, the image of the Hindu religion in India has been severely tainted by the hate campaigns led by Hindu extremists, as well as by the unjust caste system.

Christianity has not been helped either by the lack of love and grace exhibited by some ultra-fundamentalists or by the extreme liberalism of some within the mainstream churches. Moderate religious leaders, who hold true to the basic tenets of their faiths but who recognize the biblical injunction that we are not simply to coexist with but love our neighbors, can unite in the face of the extremism that damages the fabric of each faith and of our broader societies. Such a step would help break down barriers and challenge the rise of fundamentalism.

Peacemaking is a costly activity; those who engage in it risk being misunderstood by both sides, and in many contexts the danger of death is all too real. But this role is worthwhile; when there is peace, stable and free societies are created or maintained, societies in which the kingdom can grow, mature, and expand. When there are warring communities sowing hatred, on the other hand, kingdom activity can be hindered, and in some cases grind to a halt.

Who Is My Neighbor?

Immediately after Jesus informed the expert in the law that the way to inherit eternal life is to love the Lord with all our heart, soul, mind, and strength, as well as to love our neighbor as ourselves, this seeker responded with a question we may all have asked in one form or another: Who is my neighbor? Jesus replied not directly but with the well-known parable of the Good Samaritan in Luke 10:25–37.

This parable sums up the situation today. All over the world, people have been attacked, robbed, beaten, and even killed by assailants—dictators, tyrants, religious extremists, terrorists, guerrillas, and drug cartels. And throughout history, the church has produced Samaritans who have helped those who are suffering—people like Corrie ten Boom, whose family hid Jews from the Nazis. But it has also walked by on the other side of the road like the priest and the Levite.

In India, for example, the father of the Indian constitution and of the Dalit liberation movement, Dr. B. R. Ambedkar, turned to the church for help and found the doors closed to him. The caste system and caste-based discrimination were being practiced even within parts of the church. The church's leadership feared offending the upper castes and therefore refused to express solidarity with the Dalits at the time.

The church in India has also remained silent on other issues of injustice. When Indian crowds massacred Sikhs in Delhi and other places after the assassination of Prime Minister Indira Gandhi, the church did not do what it could have done to bring peace to the situation, even though individual Christian groups helped. The church's brave intervention in the Gujarat massacres of Muslims in 2002 stands out as one noteworthy instance of its getting involved in a tangible way to help persecuted non-Christians in India.

Throughout the world, the church regularly has been found to be on the wrong side of practical care and compassion. In the struggle against apartheid in South Africa, there was significant resistance from a few within the church, such as by Archbishop Desmond Tutu, but many within its fold barely raised their voices, while some even distorted theology to justify white supremacy. In the next chapter we will examine instances where the church has both succeeded and failed to act in a Christlike manner toward injustice, as well as the consequences of each approach.

Chapter Five

FOR THE RECORD

Word and Deed—Then and Now

Unguarded strength is a double weakness.

OSWALD CHAMBERS,
MY UTMOST FOR HIS HIGHEST

The church around the world has the power and means to accomplish enormous good—and devastating harm. The difference lies in the appropriate use of the Holy Spirit's power in us for God's purposes, or the inappropriate appeal to the religious spirit to dominate people and undermine God's intentions for humankind.

When Paul addressed the church in Ephesus, he made a distinction between these two spirits and their fruit:

> You were dead in your transgressions and sins, in which you used to live when you followed the ways of this world and of the ruler of the kingdom of the air, the spirit who is now at work in those who are disobedient. . . . Like the rest, we were by nature objects of wrath. But because of his great love for us, God, who is rich in mercy, made us alive with Christ even when we were dead in transgressions. . . . For it is by grace you have been saved, through faith—and this not from yourselves, it is the gift of God—not by works, so that no one can boast. *For we are God's workmanship, created in Christ Jesus to do good works, which God prepared in advance for us to do* (Ephesians 2:1–4, 8–10, emphasis added).

The history of the church is filled with examples of those who performed the "good works" that God had "prepared in advance for us to do" and those who "followed . . . the spirit who is now at work in those who are disobedient." In this chapter we will look at both brands of church members as they illustrate the issues of human rights, and especially racial equality.

The Good News about the Good News: Historical Examples

In England

Few movements of principled, Spirit-led justice are as clear and inspiring as that begun by John Wesley in England in the eighteenth century, a movement that would later lead to the founding of the The Wesleyan Church in America. John Wesley began his ministry in 1738, when he had his "Aldersgate experience" and went out to minister to many people in the open fields. After studying at Oxford—where he and other students balanced their theological studies with practical service like visiting the poor, attending the sick, and befriending the imprisoned—Wesley's ministry sparked the great spiritual awakening of the eighteenth century throughout Britain.

The result: many moral and social reforms, perhaps the most important of which was the abolition of slavery in 1772. This was partly the work of Granville Sharp, who pressed the "King's Bench" (England's Supreme Court) to make the decision that liberated slaves in England—but not in British colonies. His Lordship Judge Mansfield reported that the court agreed to do so because slavery is contrary to God's law.

Two years later, Wesley wrote his famous essay on slavery, in which he said: "Notwithstanding ten thousand laws, right is right and wrong is wrong still." Soon thereafter, a gifted young member of Parliament, William Wilberforce, took up the abolitionist cause. Just days before Wesley died in 1791, he wrote his last letter to this young Christian statesman, urging him to continue the fight. It was an almost impossible assignment, but in 1807, after 20 years of campaigning by Wilberforce, a bill to terminate the slave trade was carried by a vote of 283 to 16.

Wilberforce did influence the government to forbid British ships from engaging in the lucrative slave trade. He died in 1833, one month before Parliament passed the law liberating all slaves in the British Empire. "An indefatigable reformer and supreme abolisher of Britain's odious slave trade, Wilberforce arguably led the single most effective stand against evil and injustice in all history," reflects Os Guinness in his book *Character Counts.*[1] In his book *Saints and Society,* Dr. Earle E. Cairns has added that English evangelicals like Wesley and Wilberforce may have accomplished more for good than any single reform movement in history.

In America

In the years following the American Revolution, Virginia slave holder Colonel George Mason urged America's early leaders to abolish slavery when they were drafting the US Constitution in 1787, warning them that God would judge the

---

1. Os Guinness, *Character Counts,* p. 69.

nation if they failed to do so. Later, Presidents Washington and Jefferson were apologetic for the ancient evil of slavery and wished it to go away.

But by the 1830s, the South had begun to justify its "peculiar institution." Defenders of slavery claimed that the Bible actually approved of the practice. The situation was exacerbated in the North. In 1837, Elijah P. Lovejoy, who published an antislavery newspaper, was killed in Illinois. William Lloyd Garrison, the publisher of *The Liberator*, was dragged down the street in Boston with a rope around his body and would probably have been hanged if he had not been rescued and jailed for his own safety.

Just a decade after the death of Wilberforce, the Wesleyan church in America was born—again in service to the ideals of Christian human rights and in opposition to injustice toward African slaves. Officially formed in 1843 in Utica, New York, by a group of ministers and laymen, the new denomination broke away from the Methodist Episcopal Church, primarily over the issue of slavery.

Leaders of the new body included LaRoy Sunderlan, who had been tried and defrocked for his antislavery writings, and Luther Lee, a minister who later operated an Underground Railroad station in Syracuse, New York, an important stop along a complete network of secret routes by which African slaves from the South escaped to free states in the North with the help of such abolitionists. In obedience to Jesus' command to love God and love people, these Christian leaders and many others longed both to spread "scriptural holiness over these lands" and to secure justice for their fellow human beings. In addition to antislavery, the early Wesleyan Methodists also championed the rights of women.

The church has over the centuries included many other stalwart proponents of justice. In a speech that continues to challenge Christians today, Wilberforce declared to the House of Commons: "We can no longer plead ignorance. We cannot evade it. We may spurn it. We may kick it out of the way. But we cannot turn aside so as to avoid seeing it."[2]

Wilberforce still stands as an inspiration for Christians in politics who seek to use their position to fight injustice—individuals such as Baroness Cox and Lord Alton in the British House of Lords, as well as Representative Chris Smith, Senator Barack Obama, Senator Sam Brownback, Representative Frank Wolf, Representative Todd Akin, Representative Tom Lantos, Representative Tom Tancredo, and Representative Joseph Pittsin the United States Congress.

The Good News about the Good News: Contemporary Examples

In modern times, there have been and continue to be brave church leaders who dare to speak out, often at risk to their lives. Many of these are bishops—Archbishop Desmond Tutu in South Africa and Bishop Macram Gassis in Sudan

---

2. Ibid., p. 83.

have already been mentioned—but we can add to the list the Roman Catholic archbishop of Bulawayo in Zimbabwe, Pius Ncube; the Anglican bishop of Jos, Nigeria, Benjamin Kwashi; the Roman Catholic bishop of Hong Kong, Joseph Zen; and the martyred Catholic archbishop of San Salvador, Oscar Romero.

In 1989 another brave leader, Bishop Belo, at great personal risk, wrote a letter to the secretary general of the United Nations calling for help for the oppressed people of East Timor. In it he lamented, "We are dying as a people and a nation." And in his homily the Sunday before Archbishop Oscar Romero was killed, he addressed his message to the El Salvadoran military:

> Brothers, you are from our same *pueblo*, you kill our brother *campesinos*; and before an order to kill given by a man you ought to reflect on the law of God which says: do not kill. No soldier is obliged to obey an order that is contrary to the will of God. Nobody has to fulfill an immoral law.

> Now it is time that you recover your consciences and that you first obey your conscience rather than an order to sin. The church, defender of the rights of God, of the law of God, of the human dignity of the person, cannot remain shut up before such

an abomination. We want the government to take seriously that reforms achieved with so much blood serve no one.

In the name of God, then, and in the name of this suffering *pueblo*, whose cries rise to the heavens, every day more clamouringly, I beg, I ask, I order you in the name of God: stop the repression.[3]

Martin Luther King is another example of a Christian who has spoken out boldly against injustice—and paid the price. "As a Christian," King once declared,

you have the responsibility to stand up courageously against [unjust] laws . . . regardless of the consequences. The fear of physical death and being run out of town should not be your primary concern. Your primary concern should be a devotion to truth, justice and freedom. Often this means bearing a cross, but like Jesus you must be willing to bear it, realizing that unearned suffering is redemptive.

---

3. Susan Bergman, *A Cloud of Witnesses: 20th Century Martyrs*, pp. 68–69.

One principle that Dr. King and all the other individuals mentioned above never forgot was that we as Christians are called to love our enemies and that our struggle is not ultimately against people but against oppression itself. "The tension in this city is not between white people and Negro people," Dr. King used to point out to his audiences in Montgomery, Alabama. Going on,

> The tension is at bottom between justice and injustice, between the forces of light and the forces of darkness. And if there is a victory it will be a victory not merely for 50,000 Negroes, but a victory for justice and the forces of light. We are out to defeat injustice and not white persons who may happen to be unjust.[4]

For the Record in East Timor

Sister Maria Lourdes Martins da Cruz, sometimes known as "Mana Lou," is another person who never walks by on the other side of the street. Born in 1962 into a Catholic family in East Timor, her Christian faith came alive when at the age of four she listened to the story of the nativity from the lips of her father. When she heard that Mary and Joseph had been told

---

4. See *www.generositywithoutborders.org*.

there was no room for them in the inn, and that the baby Jesus was born in a stable, she was incensed at the injustice and went to prepare her own bedroom to receive Mary, Joseph, and the baby Jesus. Her walk with Christ found its earliest beginnings in an immediate and deep understanding of the call for his followers to fight injustice.

Throughout her teens, Maria nurtured a call to become a nun, and she spent her school holidays assisting priests around East Timor. She entered several traditional convents, seeking her vocation, and in 1985, when she was twenty-three, God spoke very directly to her. She had been extremely upset by the suffering in East Timor and had been praying almost continuously for several days at a retreat.

One day she sat in a room alone, praying. In front of her on the wall was a striking picture of the face of Jesus on the cross, the crown of thorns upon his head. A voice called out from deep within her:

> I am suffering. What will you do for me?
> Why do you spend all your time inside the
> convent? I do not live only in the convent, I
> live out there with the poor and the oppressed,
> and I need you to follow me there.

As the recipient of this startling message, Maria collapsed, unconscious, and when she came to she knew what she had to do. Maria Lourdes established the Institute of Brothers and Sisters in Christ, with a specific mission to serve the poor and oppressed. Replicas of that same picture of Christ hang in all the institute's houses around East Timor.

Sister Lourdes and the members of her institute helped many people during the days of oppression in East Timor, and now as these individuals seek to rebuild their shattered lives, she is helping the poor restore dignity to their homeland. In 1999, in the period preceding and immediately following the referendum on East Timor's independence, Sister Lourdes remained in the center of the conflict, while many others fled.

In April of that year the Indonesian military and their militia gangs slaughtered villagers hiding in the church in Liquica, throwing tear gas into the church and then shooting randomly as the panicked people poured out. The soldiers went so far as to fire rounds into the roof of the priest's house, knowing that villagers were hiding there; they left only when blood dripping through the ceiling convinced them that no one could have remained alive.

Most of the remaining village leaders and the priest fled the village after this attack, leaving many people displaced, living on the church grounds, injured, sick, hungry, and held captive by the Indonesian-backed militia. It was at this point that Sister Lourdes made her entrance. Driving, undaunted, through militia roadblocks, she revealed an extraordinary manner of communicating with the oppressors. At each roadblock she would get out of her car, fully aware that she was a target, and speak to the armed militiamen. "Within moments she would have them laughing with her, crying with her and then on their knees praying with her," recalled Dr. Daniel Murphy, an American doctor who witnessed her in action.

When the result of the UN-organized referendum was announced, and it became clear that over 80 percent of the people had chosen independence for East Timor, the Indonesian military and militia unleashed a horrific wave of violence and terror, razing 80 percent of the capital's buildings. Thousands fled the burning capital, Dili, into the surrounding hills, and an estimated 15,000 people congregated in the forest surrounding Sister Lourdes's institute.

Here she witnessed another miracle. She and her associates looked after these displaced and suffering individuals, although they did not have enough rice even for 15 people, let alone 15,000. Each morning she got up early to pray, then started cooking a barrel of rice—and for three weeks, until the very day the international peacekeeping force led by the Australians arrived, that barrel of rice never ran out.

In 1997, Sister Lourdes was awarded the international Pax Christi Award. Unable to receive it in person, she sent a message that began with these words:

> As servants of Christ, we have ideals and dreams. We would like to work with all our strength to build a new world where there will be sisterly and brotherly relations among people. We would like to help them to love

one another as true sisters and brothers in Christ.

Sister Lourdes went on to state that "the people of East Timor live in a situation and atmosphere of suppression" and that their plight was "a challenge to those who are better off, both inside the country as well as outside, to stretch out a helping hand, to support these people as much as possible." People could help in different ways, she invited, whether in the fields of development, economics, or politics. "Political help and attention is important indeed. But the main point is the question: how can we help to lift up the people to human dignity?" Sister Lourdes closed with this thought:

> In all this work we try to co-operate with whoever wants to join us. If we could succeed in this, we would be sure that peace, love, justice, truth, freedom, forgiveness and unity will be born. Peace begins with solidarity.

For the Record in Pakistan

Moving on to Pakistan, we can learn from men like retired air force Group Captain Cecil Chaudhry. Chaudhry, principal of St. Anthony's College in Lahore, is a former fighter pilot and one of the most highly decorated war heroes in Pakistan. When his name came up for promotion, however, Pakistan's then dictator General Zia ul-Haq ruled against it on the grounds that Chaudhry was a Christian. Chaudhry resigned in protest and became an outspoken champion of the religious minorities in his country. He led the struggle for the restoration of a joint electoral system, eventually succeeding in 2002.

Under the previous, separate electorate system, Muslims had been permitted to vote only for a Muslim candidate, Christians for a Christian candidate, and Hindus for a Hindu candidate, resulting in irresolvable division and complete lack of interaction among different religious communities. "[This system] resulted in a close marriage between politics and religion, because candidates were elected on religious grounds," Chaudhry explained. "It fragmented the entire population of Pakistan, violated basic political human rights, and totally disrupted the social harmony of the country. It created sectarianism, which is tearing this country apart."

Chaudhry's campaign for joint electorates developed into a broad coalition, bringing together Roman Catholics and Pentecostals and everyone in between to establish the National Christian Action Forum in 1998. A year later, the even broader Christian Organization for Social Action in Pakistan (COSAP) was formed. COSAP was instrumental in anticipating and minimizing the anti-Christian backlash in Pakistan in the immediate aftermath of September 11 and the US-led attack on Afghanistan. Social harmony committees were formed in all parishes, and Chaudhry traveled throughout the nation to address clergy and lay people and to help them prepare for the repercussions that were to come. In addition, he established a crisis group with a hotline to handle emergencies. Although some churches were attacked after the war in Afghanistan, Chaudhry believes that many potential assaults were prevented by COSAP's preemptive action.

The law that is causing the greatest discrimination and suffering in Pakistan is the notorious blasphemy law, set out in section 295 of the penal code. "No other law in the name of religion has had a more devastating and massive effect in recent years than the blasphemy law," declares the Catholic church's National Commission for Justice and Peace. Introduced by General Zia in 1985, this law prohibits blaspheming against the Prophet Mohammad, defiling the Koran, and insulting Islam. The penalty for blasphemy against the Prophet is death.

"This law is a weapon in the hands of extremists," declared one minority leader. From the creation of Pakistan in 1947 until the introduction of the blasphemy law, Muslims and Christians had lived side-by-side in relative harmony. But since 1985, the numbers of deaths, false convictions, wrongful imprisonments, torture cases, and instances of religious strife have risen significantly. Between 1986 and 2003, at least 280 cases of blasphemy were registered.

The key problem is that the law requires simply the testimony of one Muslim man against anyone else for a case to be registered. The end result is that the "blasphemy" cases often have little to do with blasphemy; accusations can be entirely falsified and used to settle scores. The vast majority of cases are actually filed against Muslims and relate to personal disputes unrelated to religion. But at least 78 Christians have been charged since the law was introduced, and once charged, even if they are acquitted, the accused are marked for life. Although the death penalty has never been carried out by the state, Islamic extremists try to take the law into their own hands. In prison, a blasphemy suspect is in constant danger and, once released, faces a lifetime in hiding.

Aslam Masih, for example, spent almost five years in jail on totally false charges, during which time he endured severe beatings and torture. A Christian sheep farmer from a village near Faisalabad, he fell victim to Muslim jealousy. First, Muslims refused to pay for their purchases from him, and then they stole all his sheep and goats. Finally, one man registered a blasphemy charge against him, accusing him of desecrating the Koran and blaspheming the Prophet. In jail, he was beaten by other prisoners with heavy canes, despite being held in solitary confinement. During his trial, 100 mullahs surrounded the court, intimidating the judge.

The scare tactics initially worked. Faced with two life sentences and a heavy fine, his case seemed almost hopeless. But through international campaigning and the hard work of his brave lawyer, Masih won his appeal in the high court and was acquitted. Now he will have to live the rest of his life in hiding, though even then he is not assured of safety. One hiding place was already discovered by extremists, who set fire to the building. Miraculously, Aslam Masih escaped to another refuge.

Others have not been as fortunate. Some remain behind bars. Naseem Bibi died in prison after a beating, while Yusuf Ali was fatally shot while in jail. Samuel Masih, lying in a hospital bed suffering from tuberculosis, was beaten by a policeman with a brick cutter and died from his injuries.

Chaudhry has led the campaign for repeal of the blasphemy laws, along with Shahbaz Bhatti, chairman of the All Pakistan Minorities Alliance. Bhatti, a devout Christian, puts his life on the line every day and has received death threats. So too has Parvez Aslam Chaudhry, a lawyer who has defended many blasphemy suspects, including Muslims. After one court hearing, Islamic extremists stopped his car, held a gun to his head, and warned, "We will never leave you. You are an enemy of Islam." Bhatti concludes: "We Christians are living among the hunting dogs. They want to see us dead."

For the Record in Latin America

Christians are rising up in courageous and life-changing ways in other parts of the world, too. For many years in Latin America evangelicals resisted human rights advocacy and social action because they saw them as being tainted with liberation theology. Believers there were influenced by Christian workers from the United States who preached a Christianity that focused entirely on heaven. These Latin American Christians were led to believe that suffering is to be expected and is not to be challenged.

At the height of the Cold War, anyone involved in social action in Latin America was regarded as a Communist, and it was viewed as almost sinful to be engaged in social action.

Over the past two decades, however, the situation has begun to change, and evangelicals have begun to take tentative steps in the direction of following the call toward involvement in social justice. In 1984, an evangelical Presbyterian church in the mountains was attacked during a worship service, and six boys were killed. Evangelicals realized they had a responsibility to speak out, and the Colombian Federation of Evangelical Churches (CEDECOL) has led the way.

CEDECOL saw the need to preach and to live out an integrated gospel. The group recognized that the gospel of Jesus Christ is not just one of words, but a good news that involves meeting people's physical, emotional, and educational needs, as Jesus did. They realized that justice and conflict resolution—for which Colombia was crying out—are biblical concepts. And they saw the need for greater church unity, for rising above denominational competitiveness. Consequently, they founded the Commission for Restoration, Life, and Peace (CRVP).

CRVP's involvement in addressing Colombia's many challenges is wide-ranging—from developing crop-substitution projects for cocaine farmers to building new communities for internally displaced people; from offering sex education and counseling for rape victims to negotiating over landmine clearance with armed groups in guerrilla-controlled areas. CRVP has been developing a human rights advocacy wing and is educating people on this issue.

Most of the staff members of CRVP are pastors and Christian workers whose first love in life is preaching the gospel. They are also people who have looked around at their congregations and communities and seen drug-related deaths of children at the hands of armed thugs; witnessed young women being lost to prostitution and poverty, desperation and misery; and realized that they could not in good conscience simply preach from the pulpit Sunday after Sunday without addressing the needs of their constituencies.

By taking a stand for justice, Colombian Christians are risking everything. Astrid Zuluaga, a CRVP regional coordinator, started to help a displaced family that was under threat from FARC, the guerrilla movement. She was able to relocate the family to a safehouse, where they thought they would be protected. FARC discovered them, however, and kidnapped the woman, whom they used as a sex slave, along with her two young boys. They then turned their attention on Astrid.

Just at that point, however, the paramilitaries—the unofficial armed wing of the government—became suspicious of Astrid, thinking she was a FARC informer. Phone calls, warnings, and intimidation followed, including death threats targeting her two young sons. Unable to determine whether the threats were coming from FARC, the paramilitaries, the government, or all three, Astrid herself was forced into hiding.

CRVP's director, Ricardo Esquivia Ballestas, was arrested by the government in 2004 and accused of being a member of FARC. Christian Solidarity Worldwide launched an international advocacy campaign on his behalf, an operation so successful that many Colombian government officials switched off their fax machines to avoid the barrage of letters.

"Your expressions of solidarity are signs of life, hope, and freedom," Ricardo wrote. He continued:

> Human rights often do not exist for those who have fallen out of favor with the Colombian authorities or the armed forces. Therefore, you understand my concern given these reported plans of detention and prosecution. Thank you for coming to my assistance. I pray that God will grant you strength and energy so that you will not grow weary in doing good.[5]

For the Record in Nepal

Nepal is another country where brave Christians are standing up for justice. A distinguished engineer by training, Dr. K. B. Rokaya founded a church in Kathmandu, where he serves as chairman of the Nepal Bible Society. He is also chairman of the Nepal Council of Churches and the pioneer of the NCC's new initiative, "Christian Efforts for Peace,

---

5. Christian Solidarity Worldwide, Urgent Action Appeal, February 4, 2004.

Justice, and Reconciliation" (CEPJAR), established in 2003 at a meeting of Christian leaders.

"This meeting came to the conclusion that Christians in the country can no longer remain passive onlookers but must work toward finding ways to bring peace, justice, and reconciliation," recalls Dr. Rokaya. CEPJAR has staged protests, marches, and press conferences, as well as initiating a new movement for religious freedom, supported by all faith communities. It is remarkable that these activities have taken place in a country where more than 11,000 people have been killed in recent years, over 1,300 people have disappeared, and the constitution prohibits religious conversions. Like so many other heroes of our faith, Dr. Rokaya is daily putting his life on the line.

* * *

We could speak too of the blind Christian human rights activist in Cuba, Juan Carlos Gonzales Leiva, who is incarcerated there. Or of the National Christian Evangelical Alliance of Sri Lanka and its bold advocacy against anti-Christian violence and proposed anti-conversion legislation in that country. Or of John Dayal of the All India Christian Council in his stellar stand against the process of extremist Hindu religious fundamentalism. But even as we reflect on these Christian examples, we are concerned about neglecting other courageous leaders in the struggle for freedom throughout the world, individuals who may or may not have had an explicit Christian faith but who nonetheless have much to teach us about fighting for dignity with dignity, about pursuing reconciliation as well as freedom.

India's Mahatma Gandhi, South Africa's Nelson Mandela, Tibet's Dalai Lama, East Timor's Xanana Gusmao, Czechoslovakia's Vaclav Havel, the Soviet Union's Alexander Solzhenitsyn, and Burma's Aung San Suu Kyi are just some people whose writings we do well to read, whose speeches we ought to digest, whose teachings we would benefit from absorbing, for they can provide a proper and healthy inspiration for us as we seek to put Christ's message into action.

The Bad News about the Good News

The Pentecostal movement in South Africa started as an association of integrated believers. But "it soon divided along color lines. In apartheid South Africa, the white Pentecostals took racial segregation a step further than their American or European counterparts," according to Dr. Nico Horn.[6] The Apostolic Faith Mission (AFM) of South Africa, for example, enforced and defended apartheid within its own movement. In 1908, the decision was taken to baptize blacks and whites separately. In 1917, the executive council decided to introduce separate places of worship. At the same meeting, it was agreed

---

6. Dr. Nico Horn, *From Human Rights to Human Wrongs: The Dramatic Round-About-Turn of the South African Pentecostal Movement on Human Rights Issues*, Birmingham, November, 2004. p. 2.

that "we do not teach or encourage social equality between Whites and Natives."

In a letter to the South African prime minister in 1956, one of the AFM's leaders, Pastor du Plessis, praised the work of Pastor G. R. Wessels and of his own brother David du Plessis for their efforts to incorporate the AFM into Afrikaner life. "Today, thank God, the AFM is a pure Afrikaner church," he wrote. Whatever his intentions, the use of such language at such a time of racial division was outrageous. Dr. Horn concludes:

> Throughout the years of Verwoerdian apartheid, the AFM never raised its voice against the crude oppression of the vast majority of the people. The forced removals of 3.5 million people, the banning of hundreds, if not thousands, without a chance to defend themselves, the detentions of thousands without trial and the vulgar implementation of the dehumanising Mixed Marriages Act and Article 16 of the Immorality Act never even raised an eyebrow among white Pentecostals. On the contrary, there are indications that the white section of the AFM actively supported the system.[7]

---

7. Ibid., p. 18.

Pastor Wessels became a National Party senator, with the AFM's blessing, in 1955. Yet even the international Pentecostal movement, according to Dr. Horn, "remained silent." That same year, Pastor Wessels was a key speaker at the International Pentecostal Conference in Stockholm. The issue of apartheid was never raised with him because, the organizers explained, "we did not want to quench the Spirit."[8]

The same was true among some groups in the United States. Certain white churches in parts of the country preached racial hatred rather than protesting against injustice. As Dr. Samuel Zalanga points out, many white evangelical Christians fiercely resisted the civil rights movement in the 1960s led by Dr. Martin Luther King. "In Lynchburg, Virginia, . . . Thomas Road Baptist Church did not allow blacks to worship there," and some preachers "made a formal theological argument attacking Martin Luther King's involvement with and leadership of the civil rights struggle."[9]

In Rwanda, some priests and nuns were found to have been involved in the slaughter of rival tribes. And in the former Yugoslavia, Serbians acted with gross brutality in the name of Orthodox Christianity.[10]

---

8. Ibid., p. 19.

9. Dr. Samuel Zalanga, *Christianity and Human Rights: The Fourth Annual Lilly Fellows Program,* November, 2004, Bethel University, USA, p. 13.

10. Geoffrey Robertson, *Crimes Against Humanity*, p. 316.

In East Timor's struggle, while the Catholic Church inside that country bravely stood with the persecuted and oppressed, the Vatican was not always reliable. When Suharto's government in Indonesia, which had invaded East Timor in 1975 and brutally occupied the territory, complained about the bishop, Dom Martinho da Costa Lopes, and his outspoken criticism of the brutal oppression perpetrated by the Indonesian military, the Vatican removed the bishop from his position and replaced him with a young priest, Dom Carlo Filipe Ximenes Belo, whom most people regarded in 1983 as more congenial toward the Indonesian occupation.

Initially, Bishop Belo was regarded as such a collaborator that some priests boycotted his consecration. But, as events turned out, Bishop Belo proved to be an even more robust critic of the oppressors than his predecessor, and for this he won the Nobel Peace Prize.

The turning point, according to Bishop Hilton Deakin, an Australian Catholic and long-term activist for East Timor, was a visit by Bishop Belo to the scene of a dreadful massacre. "When he went there, there were no villages where there had been villages, there were no people where there had been people," recalls Bishop Deakin. Bishop Belo "suddenly started walking up a hill and saw pieces of people strewn around. While he wanted to concede as much goodwill as he could to the Indonesians, this was when it changed." The Vatican could not have predicted this course of events; otherwise, it is unlikely that Bishop Belo would have been appointed.

The most significant twentieth-century failure on the part of Christ's earthly body, however, was the unwillingness of the churches in Germany and Italy to stand up against the Holocaust. It is not inconceivable that the decline of Christianity in Europe since World War II may be due, at least in part, to that failure on the part of the churches to act. When the church fails to act in truth, justice, and courage at historic times of evil against humanity, it signs its own death warrant for subsequent generations.

It is true that Hitler's Germany also had its confessing church, which protested against the atrocities—and paid the price for its boldness. Hitler liquidated Christians as well as Jews. But, if more Christian leaders of that time had challenged Hitler, as exceptional individuals such as Dietrich Bonhoeffer did so courageously, such an example would have left its imprint on history and restored moral credibility to the church. Instead, the utter silence of both the Protestant and the Roman Catholic churches, and the complicity that signing a document with Hitler entailed, demonstrated that Christianity, when it came to the test, could not stand up to the tyranny.

Each of us as a professing Christian is called to be "salt and light" in the world. As "salt" is tasted and "light" is seen, the emphasis of Jesus is on the doing and the action, not just the compassion. As our Lord himself points out in Matthew 5, salt that loses its quality of saltiness is no longer good for anything, "except to be thrown out and trampled by men." A city on a hill cannot be hidden, Jesus reflects, nor do people light a lamp and then hide it under a bowl. "Instead they put it on its stand, and it gives light to everyone in the house. In the same way, let your light shine before men, that they may see your good deeds and praise our Father in heaven."[11] We are called, each and every one of us, to take our light and shine it into the darkness.

When Cain attacked and killed his brother Abel, and the Lord asked him where Abel was, Cain lied in an attempt to wash his hands of responsibility. "I don't know," he responded. "Am I my brother's keeper?" (Genesis 4:9). God's emphatic answer was, and is, *yes*—we are all our brothers' and sisters' keepers. We all have a responsibility to penetrate the world's dark places with the light Christ has given us, to watch out for our "siblings" around the world. Christian singer Julie Carrick sums up this theme well in the convicting lyrics of her song "Where Are You?":

> *I hear the children cry, their voices raised in prayer.*
> *Will no one answer their plea?*
> *I see the people die, but you don't seem to care,*
> *You turn your heads and leave it all to me.*
>
> *Where are you? Are you lost, or are you hiding?*
> *I've been looking in the garden, but I cannot find you*
> *   there.*
> *Where is Abel? I can hear his cry arising*
> *Are you lost or are you hiding?*
> *I am still here—where are you?*

---

11. Matthew 5:13–16.

*Your hearts have hardened so my hands are
  paralyzed.*
How can I show you my mind?
I've tried to teach you how to see through other eyes
But you instead have chosen to be blind.

*Will you shepherd my flock? Will you seek to save
  the lost?*
Or will they walk there alone?
*For my yoke may seem great to you who estimate the
  cost*
But greater still is your own.

Chapter Six

WHAT NEXT?

Responding to the Need

It is infinitely difficult to begin when mere words
must remove a great block of matter. But there is no
other way if none of the material strength is on your
side. And a shout in the mountains has been known to
cause an avalanche.

ALEXANDER SOLZHENITSYN

At the Last Supper, Jesus intervened in a dispute among his disciples about which one of them was the greatest. He informed them that in the world's terms, those who exercise authority, call themselves kings or benefactors, or sit at the table being waited upon are the most prominent; but in Christ's kingdom terms, all of that is reversed. Indeed, the greatest is the one who serves. Our Lord went on to add:

> You are those who have stood by me in my trials. And I confer on you a kingdom, just as my Father conferred one on me, so that you may eat and drink at my table in my kingdom.[1]

Remembering Christ's earlier teaching on the sheep and the goats—his reference to treating the sick, feeding the hungry, welcoming the stranger, and visiting the prisoner as though serving Christ himself (Matthew 25:31–46)—it is clear from this passage in Luke that the inheritors of the kingdom are those who stand by Jesus in his trials—and that means standing by our neighbors in their tribulations.

If this point needs any reinforcement, consider Hebrews 13:3: "Remember those in prison as if you were their fellow prisoners, and those who are mistreated as if you yourselves were suffering."

---

1. Luke 22:28–29.

That we are to act in solidarity with the oppressed is not in doubt. Just as we through our relationship with Christ have an advocate in heaven, we are now called to intercede on behalf of the oppressed. Gary Haugen puts it this way: "We need to ask God to help us make it clear to the Christian community that the work of advocacy is desperately needed, thoroughly biblical, and eminently doable."[2] The third of these criteria is worth particular note.

Having read this far, the question on readers' minds may well be: Yes, but how? Advocacy appears at first complex, delicate, and daunting. Moses did not want to go to Pharoah, and we may be reluctant to mediate as well. The need for advocacy, after all, involves people who are suffering—not because they have not heard the gospel, or because they lack a church, nor specifically because of physical deprivation, though these may be symptoms. Haugen points out that people who are suffering are in a different category of need.

> They are suffering because they have an
> oppressor. They are hurting because they have
> bullies who abuse them. They are victims of
> injustice. And, for the most part, the existing
> ministries of the evangelical community do
> not provide meaningful help at their point of
> need. This, then, is the vast new frontier of
> justice advocacy. And it would be difficult to

---

2. Gary Haugen, *Justice, Mercy & Humility: Integral Mission and the Poor*, edited by Tim Chester, p. 188.

identify another area of ministry where there
is such a disparity between the magnitude of
need, the clarity of the biblical mandate, and
the dearth of actual ministry.[3]

Yet it is not as difficult as we might suspect to address this
problem and stand in the gap on others' behalf. There are a
variety of ways of fulfilling the call to be advocates, and each
of us can do our part.

Advocacy

Every one of us has a sphere of influence. For some that
area may appear more important, or broader, than for others,
but in God's terms we each have influence. Os Guinness notes
that

within our definite limits we are each
responsible. None of us can save the world,
and to try to do so would be to flirt with
despair. Our tiny circles of influence are
limited, some less so than others, but for all of
us that influence is significant. And when we
each exercise our responsible significance,
and the significance of each of our callings

---

3. Gary Haugen, *Justice, Mercy & Humility,* p. 192.

overlap with those of others, the ripples we
make together can spread far and wide.[4]

Guinness goes on to argue that each one of us

> is still always responsible for our part. Even
> in a globalised world, we are our neighbour's
> neighbour. Even in a bureaucracy, we are
> never helpless pawns but responsible agents
> who will have to give an account of ourselves
> to one who is higher than my boss. Even under
> the tyrant's threat of death, we are moral
> agents who can choose to disobey as well as
> obey. . . . None of us is without responsibility.
> To be human is to be responsible."[5]

And with that responsibility comes the *requirement* to
make a difference.

Essentially, there are two forms of advocacy, equally valid
and totally interdependent. To categorize them simply, they
can be described as *private* and *public* forms of advocacy, or,
to use other terminology, *engagement* and *protest*. In some
instances it is possible, though difficult, for one individual or
organization to combine the two. More typically, however, it
would fall to some individuals and organizations to implement

---

4. Os Guinness, *Unspeakable*, p. 236.

5. Ibid., p. 169.

a private role of engagement, and to others to take a public or perhaps confrontational approach toward the oppressors.

Before discussing the details of private and public advocacy, there are two sets of essential principles to guide our efforts on behalf of the oppressed. These may be expressed in different ways. First, we are to *pray*, *protest*, and *provide*. All three acts can be done privately or publicly, but prayer is largely private, while both protest and provision are primarily conducted publicly. Second, in the service of advocacy, three other guiding principles overlap with prayer, protest, and provision but express the same means in more depth: They are *authenticity*, *aid*, and *accountability*. We will discuss these three values later in this chapter.

Private Engagement

Prayer

Prayer must always be the starting point, and sometimes it is all we can do. But prayer is in itself a form of advocacy— it is crying out to the supreme decision maker for divine intervention. As the biblical writer points out in James 5:13–16, "Is any one of you in trouble? He should pray. Is anyone happy? He should sing songs of praise. . . . The prayer of a righteous man is powerful and effective." We are called to intercede, to pray for help, and—when we see our prayers being answered—to offer the praise and glory to God.

Prayer is the feature that distinguishes Christian human rights activism from secular activism, and it is the most effective method for confronting oppression. When Christians pray, the situation is reminiscent of Moses standing with the staff of God raised up as the Israelites fought the Amalekites (Exodus 17:8–16). When the man of God raised his hands the Israelites were on the offensive, but as soon as he lowered them they began losing ground.[6]

The same is true of us and our prayers. We are invited to intercede tirelessly for the oppressed, for those who serve them, and even for their oppressors (see Luke 23:34). And prayer need not only be personal and private, though each of us individually is to commit to praying for the oppressed. It can and should also be corporate and public; when that happens, not only is the spiritual power of prayer released, but people are made aware of the suffering and are encouraged toward further prayer and action.

So, for example, in November of every year there is a designated International Day of Prayer for the Persecuted Church, a setting in the context of which Christian human rights agencies, churches, and individuals can gather around the world to remember our persecuted brothers and sisters in prayer. There are also days and weeks of prayer set aside for specific countries. A group called Christians Concerned for Burma, for example, organizes the Global Day of Prayer for Burma on the second Sunday of every March, inspired

6. Exodus 17:8–15.

by a request from Burma's detained democracy leader, Nobel Laureate Daw Aung San Suu Kyi, who asked an American working in Burma to encourage Christians around the world to pray for that land.

For several years, Christian organizations in the UK and other countries have commemorated a Week of Prayer for North Korea. In September 2004, a Day of Prayer for Nigeria was organized, and the following year a similar event was held for Colombia. In July 2004 and 2005, churches in the north of England observed a day of prayer for Pakistan. All of these events serve to gather people spiritually and practically, to raise awareness, and to inspire new advocates and activists.

Professional Engagement

In addition to the important work of prayer, professional service at home and around the world can be another effective kind of private engagement. There are some people in the world who, through a combination of skill and opportunity, are able to build relationships with the perpetrators of injustice and oppression that can lead to improvements in the human rights situation on the ground.

A paramount Christian principle in our advocacy is that we are to seek to hear both sides of a story, that we at least attempt to talk to the oppressors and seek reconciliation. That is our role as peacemakers, as people called by our Lord to bless those very ones who persecute us (Matthew 5:43–44). There is a central role for those who choose, rather than shouting in the public square about injustice, to sit down with the accused and try to help them find a way to stop abusing their people.

This role can be fulfilled by businessmen, lawyers, diplomats, and lay church leaders. Sometimes it can be filled by people who have a track record of being outspoken. In 2003, Lord Alton, Baroness Cox, and James Mawdsley, for example, embarked on a historic visit to North Korea, despite having been uncompromisingly critical of the North Korean regime's brutal suppression of its people. Yet there they found the beginnings of the possibility of meaningful dialogue, and they have pursued that course, inviting a high-level North Korean delegation to London six months later and discussing, without holding back, the serious allegations of horrific treatment of the one million or more people held in that country's vast prison camp system. It remains to be seen whether their approach will lead to reform in North Korea, but it is an opportunity worth pursuing, given that the North Koreans have proven more willing than might have been expected to discuss these matters.

American businessman John Kamm, now based in the United States but previously a Hong Kong-based entrepreneur and chairman of the American Chamber of Commerce in Hong Kong, has used his business interests in China as a means for advocating on behalf of prisoners of conscience. Each time he travels to China on a business trip, he brings with him a list of prisoners of conscience, along with details of the prisons in which they are being held and the dates of their arrests, and he raises their cases with officials in the Chinese government. As a result of the trust and friendship he has developed with the Chinese, he has managed to secure the release of a number of prisoners.

Two Christian organizations, Advocates International, founded by Sam Ericsson, and the Institute for Global Engagement, established by the former president of World Vision, Robert Seiple, have adopted the private engagement approach. Advocates International has built a network of lawyers around the world and works to equip attorneys, including public prosecutors, with a better understanding of human rights and religious freedom. The organization works within the justice systems of the countries concerned, without involvement in public advocacy.

Similarly, the Institute for Global Engagement builds relationships with governments and then privately raises issues and cases with officials on the basis of trust. The institute does not publicly criticize oppressive regimes but instead seeks to argue, passionately but behind closed doors, the case against religious persecution and oppression. This approach has been particularly successful in Laos, which has seen significant improvements in the area of religious freedom, even though the government declared Christianity "public enemy number one" in 1999.

The engagement approach could not function without public advocacy, because there would be little leverage to influence decision makers behind closed doors if there were no pressure from outside quarters. It is also worth noting that public advocacy alone can at times be ineffective if a regime feels it has no friends to begin with. The "private-public" advocacy relationships work in tandem, and ideally in partnership.

But underpinning all advocacy, whether public or private, is the essential cornerstone of accuracy of information. All advocates, whether at a high or a grassroots level, need to be correctly informed. Credibility is everything in the area of advocacy. If an intermediary makes a mistake and gets the facts wrong, those to whom this individual is appealing for help, whether Western governments, the media, lawyers, companies, or the governments of nations where the oppression is taking place, will cease listening or at best be skeptical with regard to future exchanges. Individuals and organizations that gain a reputation for exaggeration or inaccuracy lose the right to be heard within the corridors of power.

Before undertaking any form of engagement, Christians should strive to become as well-informed as possible about the countries God places on their hearts. Read authoritative books, watch documentaries, subscribe to magazines, join the mailing lists of reputable human rights organizations, attend human rights conferences, invite speakers to your church and home groups, and above all try to meet people from the countries themselves, either those in exile in the free world or by visiting the places of persecution.

In addition to the tangible methods of engagement described above, there is the intangible but perhaps most important element in a Christian approach to human rights:

solidarity. By traveling to places of persecution, or by meeting with and offering friendship to exiles, asylum seekers, or refugees in your home country, you are offering them a touchable human hand of support. It has been said that "pity weeps and turns away; compassion looks and stretches out a hand."

Sometimes that outstretched hand can involve advocacy and aid—some practical, meaningful help. But often what is most important is simply that the hand is outstretched, that the afflicted experience friendship in their suffering, that they know they are not alone. So often in places of persecution, Christian advocates arrive to be greeted by the people with the words, "Thank God you have come. We thought the world had forgotten us."

Public Protest

Letter-writing

All of us can and should get involved in public advocacy, or protest, at one level or another. At its most basic, grassroots level, this involves letter-writing campaigns. As citizens of free, democratic nations, we enjoy the privilege of access to our political representatives. But we do well to remember that this is a privilege we are to use primarily on behalf of those who cannot speak for themselves.

Therefore, when a situation arises, perhaps concerning an individual prisoner of conscience who has been jailed for professing and practicing his or her faith or political views, in breach of the Universal Declaration of Human Rights; or possibly relating to a continuing policy or law of oppression, or to the persecution of a community, we can write to a variety of people in positions of influence.

These might include members of Parliament in the United Kingdom; representatives or senators in the United States; the foreign minister or secretary of state of our nation; the embassy of the country in which the violations are taking place; the prime minister, president, justice minister, or other appropriate officials in the country concerned; officials of international organizations such as the European Union, the Association of South-East Asian Nations, and the United Nations; multinational companies that may be doing business in the country concerned; church leaders; and other public figures.

The place to start is with our elected representatives. If we wish to write to others as well, in consultation with those leading the advocacy campaign, the effort can often prove fruitful. To save time, however, addressing an elected representative and asking him or her to raise the issue with the government of one's own country, the country where the abuses are taking place, the EU, ASEAN, or the UN, is often enough. Elected representatives are duty-bound to respond to the concerns of their constituents, and the more letters they receive about an issue the more likely they will be to take it seriously.

An official in the British Foreign and Commonwealth Office, for example, informed Christian Solidarity Worldwide that the foreign secretary had received over forty letters from members of Parliament concerning the blasphemy laws in Pakistan—a direct result of a campaign by that organization, urging its supporters to write to their parliamentary representatives on this issue. Similarly, the Conservative Party Member of Parliament for West Dorset and senior member of the Shadow Cabinet, Oliver Letwin, has taken up the cause of freedom in Burma in a significant way, directly as a result of pressure from his constituents. He reported having received so many letters about Burma that he decided to find out about the situation firsthand.

Most recently, over 200 members of Parliament—fully one-third of the House of Commons—wrote to the British foreign secretary Jack Straw after having received letters from their constituents urging the British government to support efforts to put the issue of Burma on the United Nations Security Council agenda. Despite taking some time to make a public declaration of its position, the British government did eventually inform the House of Lords in a debate that

> our position is clear: we support the involvement of the UN in helping to address Burma's problems. We also support US efforts to get the UN Security Council to address Burma. . . . We are supporting it with effort and energy and will continue to do so. We will work consistently with the

Americans on how best to achieve the goal.
We are wholly involved.[7]

They are in fact wholly involved, largely because of a sustained public campaign to ensure this outcome.

Letters to companies doing business with brutal dictatorships can also be effective. Public pressure campaigns led to the withdrawal of British American Tobacco, Premier Oil, and numerous other Western multinationals from Burma, where foreign investment funnels money into the coffers of a regime that spends almost half its budget on its military. A new campaign against the French oil company Total, a major investor in a gas pipeline in Burma, is being developed.

In some situations, writing letters to prisoners of conscience themselves can be highly effective. If such letters actually reach the prisoners, they are encouraged in knowing they are not forgotten. And even if the letters fail to make their way into the prisoners' hands, they will be opened by censors and prison officials, who at least will know that a particular case is being watched by the international community and may perhaps be inclined on that basis to treat the prisoner with more care than might otherwise have been the case. That is not always true, and in some cases letters are not helpful, but advocacy organizations can provide information on a case-by-case basis.

---

7. Hansard, House of Lords, November 28, 2005.

One prisoner of conscience who was blessed to receive letters from people in the UK and around the world during his incarceration was Francisco Miranda Branco, an East Timorese prisoner of conscience sentenced to 15 years in jail in Indonesia for his part in organizing the march to the Santa Cruz cemetery in Dili, East Timor, in 1991 to protest the killing of a young man, Sebastian Gomes, by Indonesian military personnel on the steps of the Motael Church. Hundreds of unarmed, peaceful civilians marched from the church to the cemetery to place flowers on Gomes's grave, and as they walked they unfurled banners calling for justice and freedom. When the protestors arrived at the cemetery, however, they were surrounded by Indonesian military, who opened fire. Over 200 people were killed.

Francisco was sentenced to 15 years, and Gregorio da Cunha Saldanha, the leader of the march, was given a life sentence. The two shared a cell, and they later recalled that letters from Christians around the world, as well as the knowledge that these diverse believers were praying for them, fortified them with the strength to carry on. In one memorable reply to an activist in the UK, Francisco wrote,

> My brother, God is very kind and just, and he loves us, you and me who believe in Him. We can never feel angry and upset at God when we suffer, because behind all the suffering He has a beautiful surprise for us.

The ability to pen such words from the darkness of a prison cell is an amazing testimony of faith, but also of the power of encouragement the letters he had received had provided.

In 2004, Christian Solidarity Worldwide decided to mark the fifty-ninth birthday of Burma's democracy leader, Aung San Suu Kyi, who was still under house arrest, by urging supporters to send birthday cards to her in Rangoon. Over 200 cards were sent, including some from ten-year-old school children in Brussels. The teacher who had supervised the young students stated, "The children were full of suggestions for stopping the cruelties of the Burma Army. It would be good if some adults would see as clearly."

One child wrote, "Happy Birthday to you, Aung San Suu Kyi. We offer you hope, support and all the love from Belgium." Another affirmed, "You are a wonderful lady and you are full of courage. In the end everything you have done will turn out to make a difference. I hope you are soon freed." In another card, a child wrote, "Happy Birthday!" adding the postscript, "If a Burmese soldier opens this, [I] protest: 'Stop the War.'"[8]

Even if these cards are never received by Aung San Suu Kyi, she knows about them because the BBC, Voice of America, and Radio Free Asia all reported on the initiative and broadcast into Burma, and it is widely known that the democracy leader

---

8. Christian Solidarity Worldwide, "Hundreds of birthday cards sent to Nobel Laureate; UK Parliamentarians express solidarity," Press release, June 16, 2004—see *www.csw.org.uk*.

listens to these radio stations. Moreover, the censors who received the cards may well have been overwhelmed by the number, depth, and quality of the messages. It is our prayer that some of their hearts may have been changed as a result.

Demonstration

The second form of public protest is demonstration. The format may vary, perhaps involving a march, a protest outside an embassy, or a candlelit vigil. Demonstrations can be simple or highly creative. They can involve the delivery of a letter or petition, perhaps by a prominent politician or public figure to an embassy or company, or they can simply involve speeches and chanting from activists.

In a demonstration outside the Burmese embassy in London in August 2004, in memory of the August 8, 1988, Burmese student uprising that resulted in a massacre of thousands, protestors held up a map of Burma in chains, a life-size cage containing pictures of detained democracy leaders Daw Aung San Suu Kyi and Min Ko Naing, placards with slogans such as "Stop the Rape" and "End Use of Child Soldiers," and pictures of land mine victims and people in forced labor. Christians stood alongside Buddhists, Muslims, and atheists in that protest. An attempt was made to deliver to the embassy a box of reports documenting the violations of human rights in Burma, but the embassy staff refused to receive it.

Similarly, earlier in 2004 a demonstration was held by Christians outside the Vietnamese embassy in London in protest against the detention of Christians in Vietnam. In it, two Christian parliamentarians, Lord Chan and David Drew, tried to deliver a petition to the embassy, but again officials refused to receive it. In a protest in Hong Kong in 1999 outside the Indonesian consulate, however, the door opened a crack and a hand emerged to snatch a petition, which urged the Indonesian government to stop the slaughter of East Timorese following the referendum—hardly a gracious acceptance, but nevertheless the message was delivered.

Readers may question the effectiveness, or in some cases even the appropriateness, of demonstrations. Our response would be that one demonstration by itself is unlikely to change a situation. As one component of a wider campaign, however, protests can be highly effective. Their efficacy depends upon planning and organizing. If the numbers of participants are low, and the protest is colorless, lifeless, or poorly timed, it will have little effect, either on the target of the protest or on passersby.

If a large number of people gather, however, and if the banners, props, and speeches are bright, colorful, imaginative, and attractive and the timing correct, the impact can be significant. Timing is crucial—a protest should ideally coincide with either an important news development in the country or a recognized anniversary, and it should be scheduled for the time of day when maximum attention can be given, such as during lunchtime. Working people who might wish to participate can slip out for an hour during their lunch breaks to join in, and passersby on their way to or from lunch may see the protest and find their awareness and interest piqued. If the protest is particularly well-timed or creative, and especially if a prominent personality is involved, the media may give it some attention.

At the very least, a demonstration constitutes a gesture of solidarity to the oppressed people of a particular country, a public declaration of support that can only serve to invigorate the campaign for justice within that country. If the relevant language services of the BBC, Voice of America, and other media channels report on the demonstration, and especially if they broadcast that news into the country concerned, the oppressed people on the ground can find reassurance in the fact they are receiving moral support from around the world.

Christians do well always to be prepared to protest alongside people of other faiths, or of no faith, if there is a common interest. Sometimes, if the scenario relates exclusively to the persecution of Christians, participants in the demonstration may be exclusively Christian. But if others recognize that a wider human rights issue is involved, they may join in. And Christians are more likely to receive support for campaigns for persecuted Christians if, in turn, they support others' crusades for justice. The only requirement for Christian participation should be that the demonstration be nonviolent, orderly, and within the confines of the law.

Letter-writing and demonstrating within one's home country are perhaps the most conventional forms of public protest. We would like to propose here that the church in the free world engage more actively in these activities but also consider moving beyond them into a bolder form of action. The gospel message is bold, warning of risks and calling for sacrifice, and the life of Christian activism should follow this paradigm as closely as possible.

Protesting in one's home country is important and valid, but it is also for the most part risk-free. If we live in a democracy, we will not be arrested for demonstrating, provided the protest is organized in an appropriate manner and the participants abide by the law and coordinate the event with the police in advance. But a far more effective gesture of solidarity would be to travel to a country troubled by persecution and, in an entirely nonviolent, even spiritual way, to stage an action that declares to the authorities, as well as to our persecuted brothers and sisters in that land, that we care about those who are suffering injustice.

A precedent for this was set when a young Christian, James Mawdsley, demonstrated three times in Rangoon, the capital of Burma, as well as in Moulmein, against the oppression of the people in that country. On the first occasion, he was expelled from the country within a few days, while on the second occasion he was imprisoned for three months. On the third, he received a 17-year sentence, of which he served 14 months in solitary confinement.

We may not all be called to endure imprisonment, but Jesus was uncompromising when he declared, "Greater love has no one than this, that he lay down his life for his friends"[9] That does not imply that we all need to be martyrs or prisoners, but it does signify that we need to be prepared to make sacrifices in our lives for the sake of others and to follow our call of conscience. If tens, hundreds, even thousands of Christians were to substantiate their presence in the country containing the oppression by protesting, in various forms, the effect would be profound, confusing and shattering the confidence of the oppressors, and emboldening the oppressed.

If Christians, especially Asians in Asia and Africans in Africa, were to rise up and travel to neighboring countries where people are enslaved and imprisoned, delivering letters of protest, seeking to visit the incarcerated, staging candlelit prayer vigils and silent demonstrations, these actions would shine a light where the darkness fears it most. European and North American Christians are urged to participate as well, but the effect would be most powerful if the demonstrators were individuals from the same continent; otherwise, the demonstration could too easily be dismissed as a Western, imperialist, colonialist plot.

Europeans and Americans are hampered by their colonial histories, and although this should not hinder them from acting, they need to proceed in concert with local people. So if ordinary Thais, Japanese, Filipinos, Indonesians, Indians, Chinese, Singaporeans, and Koreans were to travel to Burma and North Korea; if Nigerians, Egyptians, Kenyans,

---

9. John 15:13.

Tanzanians, Ugandans, Tunisians, and South Africans were to demonstrate in Sudan and Zimbabwe, think what a powerful statement that would make!

Some might argue that to travel to another country to stage a protest, or indeed to investigate human rights violations without the knowledge or approval of that country's government—especially if the action involves crossing the border illegally—is a violation of the sovereignty of that land and therefore outside the realm of appropriate Christian engagement. But it is our belief that sovereignty has been wrongly defined, and that it is, in a legal, political, and spiritual sense, with the people not with their government. When the people choose their leaders and rulers through whatever mechanism they accept, and when their government treats them with dignity, the citizens have delegated their sovereignty to the government, and the laws of that government are to be respected.

However, when a government takes power by force, against the will of the people, and especially when the will of the citizenry is clearly expressed and is still ignored by the government, and when that government brutally suppresses all opposition, it has forfeited its sovereignty and should be treated accordingly. As Rafael Lemkin, the man who defined the word *genocide*, has said: "Sovereignty cannot be conceived as the right to kill millions of innocent people."[10]

---

10. Samantha Power, *A Problem from Hell*, p. 19.

Tyrants tend to be arrogant, display confidence, and appear well-armed, but their rule is ultimately based on fear. They are like Sauron in *The Lord of the Rings*, who "is not so mighty yet that he is above fear; nay, doubt ever gnaws him."[11] Tyrants rule by fear precisely because they are filled with it. They are afraid of any dissent, opposition, or challenge that might compromise their grip on power. The Christian community's private commitment to prayer and public commitment to letter-writing and demonstration can serve to break the spirit of tyrants and their minions.

Provision

A combination of prayer, protest, and provision proves to be a powerful tool in the hands of God and his people. Provision can involve time (volunteering with a human rights organization); financial sacrifice (making charitable donations to an organization, either for its general fund or earmarked for a specific country, project, or campaign); material assistance; the donation of books, clothing, medicine, and other supplies needed by the oppressed; or providing expertise in fields such as law, computer technology, medicine, language, construction, land mine clearance, or agriculture, either in one's home country or in places of persecution around the globe.

A more conventional but no less important way of providing aid and comfort to those in need is for Christians to pursue careers within the systems of influence in all free,

---

11. J. R. R. Tolkien, *The Lord of the Rings*, p. 763.

democratic, Western societies, to use positions of influence for advocacy. If more Christians were to seek elected office in the parliaments and congresses of the free world, to opt to serve as voices for the voiceless, following Wilberforce's example, the cause of freedom and justice would be significantly advanced.

Mediating within the political arena should not just entail legislating; rather, such politicians can use their influence to actively, consistently, and persistently raise the cases of individuals and communities suffering persecution and, most importantly, travel to the places of oppression to see the situations for themselves. Setting an example by speaking out, acting, and witnessing circumstances firsthand constitutes a powerful way of advocating from within the political arena.

There is also a desperate need for more Christians with a heart for justice to enter into public service, particularly in the British Foreign and Commonwealth Office, the US State Department, regional bodies such as the European Union and the Association of South-East Asian Nations, the World Bank, the International Monetary Fund, and the United Nations. Although these organizations themselves are vast bureaucracies that often fail to inspire confidence, there are notable examples of diplomats and public servants from within their ranks who have, indeed, made a difference.

Raoul Wallenberg, the Swedish diplomat who went to Hungary in 1944 with a secret but straightforward mission—

to rescue Jews from the Holocaust—is a prime example. "He pursued the hunted and the doomed with the passion of a man 'commissioned by God,'" writes Danny Smith in his biography of Wallenberg.[12]

A Christian in the US State Department was sent to Thailand to investigate claims that the Burma Army was participating in widespread rape against the Shan people. The claims were first documented in a report by the Shan Human Rights Foundation and the Shan Women's Action Network, titled *Licence to Rape*, and were verified by the US State Department as a result of this one official's research. As God intends it, the primary focus for Christians is to be the world, and if we refuse to engage in political and public service, we are handing those areas over to the enemy without so much as a fight.

The same is true of the media, an area in which there is a desperate need for Christians who will produce newspaper and magazine reports and articles, television documentaries, Hollywood films, radio programs, and songs for the secular world that highlight injustice and challenge people to action. David Aikman, former *TIME* magazine senior correspondent and author of a book about Christianity in China titled *Jesus in Beijing*, is an excellent example of a Christian who has used his career in the secular media to great effect.

---

12. Danny Smith, *Lost Hero: Raoul Wallenberg's Dramatic Quest to Save the Jews of Hungary*, p. 6.

Advocacy's Means:
Authenticity, Aid, and Accountability

This leads to the second set of values, which overlap with prayer, protest, and provision but express the same ideas in more depth. These principles constitute the modus operandi of Baroness Caroline Cox, a tireless champion of the persecuted and oppressed around the world and a member of the British House of Lords. Effective advocacy must be characterized by three key values: *authenticity*, *aid*, and *accountability*.

In Baroness Cox's view, advocacy needs to be grounded in the *authenticity* of firsthand evidence—which means, whenever possible, going to the places of persecution to see the suffering for oneself, standing alongside the people in their darkest hour, taking firsthand testimonies and recording accounts of human rights violations, collecting video and photographic evidence and other documentation, and returning to the free world with the declaration, "I have been; I have seen; this is how it really is."

Aid, as a component of advocacy, comes into play in association with authenticity because it is impossible for Christ's followers to go to a place where the people are sick and have no medicine, hungry and have no food, cold and have no clothes, homeless and have no shelter, and do nothing to meet their physical needs. As James 2:15–16 expresses it,

> Suppose a brother or sister is without clothes
> and daily food. If one of you says to him,

"Go, I wish you well; keep warm and well fed," but does nothing about his physical needs, what good is it?

An individual acting alone may not be able to do much, but, even so, a little can go a long way. It is an imperative feature of Christian human rights—and something that distinguishes the Christian program from a secular approach—that fact-finding teams entering places of persecution do not travel empty-handed. Under the auspices of Christian Solidarity Worldwide, for example, teams that visit the persecuted and oppressed often represent a mix of complementary skills— advocacy, political knowledge, international law, medicine, and media, for example—and alongside the interviewing and fact-finding, the team might also conduct medical training or offer medical consultation.

The group also brings a small financial gift—a few hundred or thousand dollars—to donate as an emergency provision to combat any urgent need they may encounter during the course of their visit—a village that has run out of food, a clinic that has been destroyed, a church that has been burned down, a community that has no medicine. And, in some parts of the world, the organization provides continuing support to selected small-scale, locally-run projects that work with the most cut-off, forgotten, needy individuals, such as the internally displaced people inside Burma, refugees and orphans on the Thai-Burmese border, or human rights advocates in Peru and Colombia. Other Christian human rights organizations, such as the advocacy group Jubilee Campaign and its sister aid organization Jubilee Action, Open Doors, Voice of the Martyrs, Release International, and Sow Hope have similar principles.

Accountability supports the other three principles. A Christian human rights organization must be accountable for its actions and expenditures, both to the supporters—those who make the work possible through financial giving—and to the oppressed—those for whom the advocates speak and act. It is crucial that advocates listen to their sources among the persecuted and oppressed on the ground in the countries about which they are speaking and that they make certain to transmit accurate information, details that the persecuted people themselves want conveyed in the manner they wish to have it presented.

In some situations media attention can be helpful; in such instances a human rights advocate can issue a press release or a report; conduct television, radio, and/or newspaper interviews (both secular and Christian); and thereby raise public awareness to the plight of a particular individual or community. However, in other situations media attention can serve to intensify the oppression and cause a backlash for the people who are already suffering. Consulting with the intended beneficiaries on the type of advocacy that is appropriate and sensitive to the needs of the situation is essential.

One final thought: Whether our efforts take the form of private engagement or public activism, the focus must be on working for justice, not on worrying about the results. Of course we need, as best we can, to ensure that we are using the most effective methods possible. But the timing of the results is not, ultimately, in our hands. As Aung San Suu Kyi appeals in her book *Freedom from Fear*,

> Don't think about whether these things [justice and freedom] will happen. Just continue to do what you believe is right. Later on the fruits of what you do will become apparent on their own. One's responsibility is to do the right thing.[13]

As you reflect on this, ask God to show you which countries he wants you to especially advocate for, and in what specific ways he is asking you to pray, protest, and provide. As you do so, make the following words your prayer—for yourself, your church, and the kingdom:

> *Let us open the clenched fist, and extend the open palm;*
> *Let us mourn, until others are comforted,*
> *Weep, till others laugh.*
> *Let us be sleepless, till all can sleep untroubled.*
> *Let us be frugal, till all are filled.*
> *Let us give, till all have received.*

13. Aung San Suu Kyi, *The Role of the Citizen in the Struggle for Democracy*, published in *Freedom from Fear*, p. 212.

Let us make no claim, till all have had their due.
Let us be slaves, till all are free.
Let us lay down our lives, till all have life
  abundantly.

Chapter Seven

NEVER GIVE UP!

The Root and Fruit of Freedom

Communism went against life, against man's
fundamental needs, against the need for freedom, the
need to be enterprising, to associate freely against
the will of the nation. . . . Something that goes
against life may last a long time, but sooner or later
it will collapse.

VACLAV HAVEL

It was midnight when the national anthem started to play for the first time. The flag was raised, and the world's newest nation—and also Asia's poorest—was born. After four hundred years of Portuguese colonial rule; twenty-four years of brutal Indonesian occupation, in which over a third of the population died; and three years of United Nations transitional administration, the people of East Timor—or the Democratic Republic of Timor-Leste—were free.

For all who witnessed the celebration in person, it was an emotional time. One man in the crowd spoke for his people, though in quiet conversation with his neighbor. He had been the first of the East Timorese to have been forcibly exiled by the Indonesians. For twenty-four years he had been unable to return home. He was a Catholic priest, Father Francisco Maria Fernandes. Asked whether he had believed he would live to see this day, he smiled and nodded. "Yes," he responded quietly, going on to elaborate:

> Throughout our struggle, people all over the world asked me: "Why do you carry on? You are fighting a losing battle. Indonesia will never let you go; the world will never help you. Why don't you just give up?" But we had one thing those people did not know about. We trusted God. This was a victory of faith.

Another East Timorese citizen, Father Domingos Soares, known as "Father Maubere," a man who had risked his life providing food and spiritual support to the resistance during the occupation, described his nation's freedom as "a miracle of solidarity." There had been many examples of divine intervention during the struggle, he pointed out, but the greatest miracle of all was attaining freedom. It had come at a high price—the Indonesians had warned the people that if they were to vote for independence in the referendum in 1999, "blood will run like rivers," and that dire prediction had proved to be only too true. "But," continued Father Domingos simply, "this is the land God gave us."

The experience of South Africa, or of the former Soviet satellite countries in Eastern Europe, shouts the same message as that of East Timor: *Never give up!* Indeed, if we exhibit courage, determination, sacrifice, persistence, prayer, and hard work, we will see victories of faith in many other places of oppression. As Jesus expressed it in Matthew 7:7–8:

> Ask and it will be given to you; seek and you will find; knock and the door will be opened to you. For everyone who asks receives; he who seeks finds; and to him who knocks, the door will be opened.

Our Lord continued in verses 9–12:

> Which of you, if his son asks for bread, will
> give him a stone? Or if he asks for a fish, will
> give him a snake? If you, then, though you
> are evil, know how to give good gifts to your
> children, how much more will your Father
> in heaven give good gifts to those who ask
> him! So in everything, do to others what you
> would have them to do you, for this sums up
> the Law and the Prophets.

Sometimes the task seems too formidable. Sometimes
it seems impossible. Sometimes success seems like nothing
more than a dream. We scarcely dare to envision that Burma,
China, North Korea, Saudi Arabia, Iran, and Cuba might one
day all be free. But we do well to hold on to words spoken
by the Chinese dissident Wang Dan, one of the leaders of the
Tiananmen Square uprising in 1989:

> I dream of a day in China when the ideas
> of freedom, democracy, human sympathy,
> tolerance and equality have pervaded
> people's hearts and minds and have radically
> transformed the patterns of social life. When
> that day comes, we can cease our tears, forget
> every painful memory and watch China
> advance toward a magnificent and brilliant

new day. If we all work hard for that day to come, it will, I believe, come.[1]

The parable of the persistent widow in Luke 18 reinforces this principle. Interestingly, Jesus concludes this passage with a challenge to every believer: "However, when the Son of Man comes, will he find faith on the earth?"

If we give up, if we stop trusting God, if we conclude that all prayer and all effort is fruitless and the struggle is over, we have already lost. But if, like the persistent widow, we continue, praying and working ceaselessly, we will see results.

As Christians, we have an eternal hope, a hope that is at the center not only of our spiritual lives and the salvation of our souls, but also of our struggle for justice in this world. All freedom comes from God. In John 10:10, Jesus declares that the "thief comes only to steal and kill and destroy; I have come that they may have life, and have it to the full." And in Galatians 5:1, the apostle Paul asserts: "It is for freedom that Christ has set us free. Stand firm, then, and do not let yourselves be burdened again by a yoke of slavery." In Romans 8:18–25, our hope is expressed in these resounding words:

> I consider that our present sufferings are not worth comparing with the glory that will be revealed in us. The creation waits

---

1. Wang Dan, Press statement, New York, April 23, 1998.

in eager expectation for the sons of God to be revealed. For the creation was subjected to frustration, not by its own choice, but by the will of the one who subjected it, in hope that the creation itself will be liberated from its bondage to decay and brought into the glorious freedom of the children of God. . . . For in this hope we were saved. But hope that is seen is no hope at all. Who hopes for what he already has? But if we hope for what we do not yet have, we wait for it patiently.

Whittaker Chambers describes communism—and all forms of dictatorship, despotism, and tyranny—as "slavery to men" and "spiritual night to the human mind and soul." He claims that freedom is "a need of the soul, and nothing else." God alone, he adds, is "the inciter and guarantor" of freedom. Chambers goes on:

It is in striving toward God that the soul strives continually after a condition of freedom. . . . He is the only guarantor. . . . Political freedom, as the Western world has known it, is only a political reading of the Bible. . . . Hence every sincere break with Communism is a religious experience. . . . A communist breaks because he must choose at last between irreconcilable opposites—

God or Man, Soul or Mind, Freedom or Communism.[2]

Ronald Reagan, for whom Chambers was an inspiration, believed that "freedom is the universal right of all God's children. . . . The cause of freedom is the cause of God. . . . I believe God intended for us to be free."[3]

In some situations change has been slow to come. Apartheid in South Africa and the stranglehold of the Soviet bloc lasted for decades. In comparison, East Timor's struggle, while it involved a bloody 24 years in which many lost their lives, was comparatively brief. But in some cases, if Christians wake up and mobilize quickly enough, a situation can be radically changed almost overnight, before too much damage is done. That happened in India in the elections in 2004.

The BJP, which had been in control of the government since 1997, was expected to be reelected in 2004. This was the party that had presided over India's economic revitalization and had attracted considerable inward investment. But it was also a Hindu nationalist party with close ties to extremist groups. The BJP was largely responsible for creating an atmosphere in India in which secularism, which had kept the country's diverse religious groups functioning in relative

---

2. Whittaker Chambers, *Witness*, pp. 16–17, as quoted in *God and Ronald Reagan: A Spiritual Life*, Paul Kengor, pp. 85–86.

3. *God and Ronald Reagan*, Paul Kengor, p. 216.

harmony for many years, was destroyed and religious hatred allowed to foment.

But just in time civil society, including the church, woke up. Commentators now say that nongovernmental organizations, civil rights groups, the village masses, the Dalits, and the Christians all played significant roles in bringing down the BJP-led government and electing the much more moderate, Congress-led United Progress Front Party (or UPA), which is committed to restoring secular society—a situation in which all religious groups are granted respect. Already the situation has changed. Anti-Christian violence has not entirely ended, and the extremists are still at large, but state-sponsored hatred is being reversed. The anti-conversion law in Tamil Nadu was overturned.

This election result sent a stark message to India's elite, a statement that the ordinary people would not be taken for granted. When consciences are awakened and people act in unity, unexpected change can indeed result. Would this reawakening have occurred if there had been no proactive human rights advocates and activists among the Christian community, no catalysts to mobilize one million people to pray for the election? Almost certainly not.

The struggle for justice in India, for Christians under persecution, and for Dalits and other oppressed groups with whom the All India Christian Council has discovered a new solidarity, forced believers from the fringes into the heart of Indian society, thereby fulfilling Christ's command to act as salt and light. This in turn caused many Indians who had been taken in by the nationalistic rhetoric of the extremists to realize that Christians were not simply out to convert everyone else, not simply bent on adding to their numbers in the pews—but rather that Christians genuinely cared about Indian society, that there is no incompatibility between being a Christian and being an Indian.

The darkness in India has lifted a little, at least for a while. But the struggle is not yet over. The struggle for Dalit rights, religious freedom, and women's rights goes on. The battle against human trafficking, the sex trade, and bonded child labor is still being waged. The fight against unjust laws and structures has not ceased. The militant Bajrang Dal and its Raksha Sena (Defense Army) are already establishing armed militias that are being trained and sent out specifically to prevent conversions to Christianity, as well as to target the Muslims.[4] But a significant victory has been won—an example of what can be achieved through prayer and concerted action by Christians committed to justice.

Christian involvement in the struggle for freedom should always, as far as possible, be nonviolent. The examples of Dr. Martin Luther King, Mahatma Gandhi, and Aung San Suu Kyi teach us the value of this principle. Dictators, however brutally they butcher and kill, are in the final analysis cowards. If sufficient critical mass and critical resistance is built, it is frequently true that a dictator can be overthrown peacefully. The end of apartheid in South Africa was not free of violent

---

4. Intercessors Network, July 17, 2004.

resistance, but ultimately this policy was overthrown not by the terrorist activities of some in the African National Congress (ANC) but by the moral pressure of the international community and the recognition by F. W. de Klerk that the system was unsustainable.

Similarly, the Soviet empire crumbled primarily through the domino effect of an uprising of the people across Eastern Europe. Milosevic, Suharto, and Marcos were all toppled by largely nonviolent people power. Once again, the image we have created of dictators being impregnable is frequently untrue.

It should be acknowledged that there have been Christians who have taken up arms to defend themselves. This issue is an area in which Christian human rights activists are divided. Either way, it would be inappropriate to pass judgment on Christians who have taken up arms to defend their own. Such believers rightly view the defense of their children, wives, and other loved ones as part of their Christian responsibility. When the enemy helps himself to your territory, rapes your women, enslaves your children, and kills your men, a last-resort violent defense of your own people is indeed understandable.

The Karen people in Burma, for example, have been fighting for survival for over half a century in the world's longest-running civil war. But their armed forces, the Karen National Liberation Army (KNLA), many of whom are Christians who enter the war zones with an M16 on their back and a Bible in their pocket, are fighting to protect their people. They are not the aggressors. As a KNLA commander once asserted, "We fight with love, not with hate. We fight simply to defend our people."

Dietrich Bonhoeffer was executed because of his involvement in a plot to assassinate Adolf Hitler. How do we reconcile that with the Christian principle of nonviolence? Bonhoeffer was a brave, moral, inspiring man. In the exceptional situation in which he found himself, though, the assassination of one individual could well have been the key to changing a horrendous situation and preventing the deaths of millions of additional victims. As such, could his intention not have been justified as an act of defense?

After Regime Change, What?

Once freedom has been attained, what next? When a struggle to overthrow an unjust system has been won, can Christians in that society rest? No. As soon as an oppressive regime is toppled, there are fresh challenges. The new struggle may be against poverty, illiteracy, disease, or unemployment. It may be a battle for justice and reconciliation or an effort to ensure that the replacement for the previous administration does not simply become another oppressive regime, maybe even worse than the first. Solzhenitsyn has pointed out that "the line separating good and evil passes not through states, not between classes, nor between political parties either—but through every human heart—and through all human hearts." The desire for retribution, or for absolute power, may well rear its ugly head to tempt the new rulers—and it must be combated.

But to prevent the desire for revenge—or feelings of hatred—from surfacing later, reconciliation must be the goal, and it has to involve much more than simply forgiving and forgetting the oppressors' acts. It means facing them— victim and perpetrator together. South Africa's Truth and Reconciliation Commission, led by Archbishop Desmond Tutu, provides a good basis for this principle, as does East Timor's. Father Domingos in East Timor set out the case for justice and reconciliation clearly: "There is no way for reconciliation without justice. Even with the Cross, there is justice—Jesus paid the price for us," he asserted. "There must be confession, apology, dialogue. Without justice, there can be no reconciliation." Justice in this context does not, however, mean retribution, or even necessarily punishment. It means simply that the perpetrators and victims "sit down together and see the truth."

A preacher once stated that God is looking for a people who dare to dream the impossible and then to ask, "Why not?" We live in a cynical society, a pessimistic society, even within the church. Many Christians are like Denethor, in the Siege of Gondor in *The Lord of the Rings*. When his land came under attack from the orcs and other soldiers of the Dark Lord of Mordor, Denethor conceded quickly in his spirit. "I will go now to my pyre. To my pyre! . . . We will burn like heathen kings before ever a ship sailed hither from the West," he predicted and, speaking of his son Faramir, who lay sick:

"He is burning, already burning. . . . The house of his spirit crumbles." Then he turned to the hobbit, Pippin, who had been in his service, and instructed, as though to confirm his defeatism: "Go now, and die in what way seems best to you."

The church needs more Christians with little Pippin's spirit. We need more hobbits—more ordinary people with extraordinary courage. "I will not take your leave, sir, for I want to see Gandalf very much indeed. But he is no fool; and I will not think of dying until he despairs of life," responded Pippin.[5] We too must not think of giving up until our Lord despairs of life—and since God is the author and giver of life, we cannot lose hope.

Tell someone that you are actively working to bring about the end of illegal, brutal military regimes like the one in Burma, and your declaration will most likely be met with incredulity. If you were claiming to be able to do all that on your own, this reaction would be valid. But as Christians we never claim the ability to do anything in our own strength. We act in partnership with others, together empowered by God's Holy Spirit. It is God who performs the wonders, using us simply as his instruments. And he is a God of miracles, perfectly capable of changing the hearts or removing from power the leaders of brutal regimes, just as he once transformed the heart of Saul on the road to Damascus (Acts 9:1–19).

5. J. R. R. Tolkien, *The Lord of the Rings*, p. 807.

So when T. E. Lawrence refers to the "dreamers of the day"—the dangerous people who act their dreams into reality "with open eyes"[6]—he could be speaking of the potential of the church, if we are to wake up. If the Berlin Wall could fall, the Soviet empire collapse, apartheid in South Africa be abolished, a moderate government be elected in India to replace the extremist regime, and Indonesia's brutal occupation of East Timor be brought to an end—why not ask, "Why not?" to the ideal of freedom and justice in other nations?

Why not be like Frodo and Sam in their quest to destroy the ring in Mordor? We may on our own be like pint-sized hobbits, with little cause for hope in the face of thousands of brutal, heavily armed orcs—but if we stick together and keep our fellowship united—and, above all, remain securely bonded to our Lord—we are bound to triumph in the end.

When a country is liberated from oppression, or when an individual prisoner of conscience is freed, there is surely jubilation in the heavenly realms, and the King of glory is invited in. As the psalmist expresses it in Psalm 24:7–8, we need to call out to the lands that are currently under the darkness of oppression:

> *Lift up your heads, O you gates;*
> *Be lifted up, you ancient doors,*
> *That the King of glory may come in.*

---

6. T.E. Lawrence, *The Seven Pillars of Wisdom.*

Who is this King of glory?
The Lord, strong and mighty
The Lord, mighty in battle.

Chapter Eight

FAITH IN ACTION

A New Beginning

This is not the conclusion of an incident, but a new
beginning. Lies written in ink can never disguise
facts written in blood.

LU XUN

The key word for our purpose is *integration*. Kingdom
mission integrates all areas of life with the life of an individual
human being or community. The poor, the disenfranchised,

and the oppressed appeal to us, "If you really care about us, why don't you do something about the conditions and systems that cause our poverty, our dehumanization, our oppression? Or are you also afraid of the systems and those who control them? Doesn't your gospel of Jesus challenge evil and the evildoers in this world?"

The critical part of the Great Commission is the discipling of all peoples. This takes place when we teach people to obey *all* that Jesus commanded and taught. Has the church reneged on Christ's commission by focusing too much attention on the teachings of Jesus that are palatable, comfortable, and inexpensive? For example, does not the Great Commission include the teaching and obeying of the Great Commandment (Matthew 22:37–40)? The Great Commission must always go hand in hand with the Great Commandment, and the Great Commandment is deeply linked with the need for involvement in the lives of those who are being oppressed, persecuted, abused, and dehumanized.

We pause here to ask a difficult question: Can the "evangel" coexist with racism, corruption, apartheid, economic exploitation, colonization, caste discrimination, paternalism, dehumanization, and the oppression of women through the sex trade and various other means? Is it possible that the principal reason why the church has failed to make disciples of all nations, teaching others to obey everything Christ has commanded, is that the church itself has in so many ways failed to live and teach fully all that Christ commanded in these areas?

Christian workers have, in some instances, stood silent in the face of grave injustice because of a hesitancy to get mixed up in "politics"—preferring to limit their sphere of activity to that of "preaching the gospel." But what good is it to preach the gospel if our actions contradict the very heart of the message of hope we are promoting? There is far too much dissonance in the presentation of the good news. People believe what they see and experience more than what they hear. What we say frequently fails to match what we do. James 1:22 is convicting in this regard: "Do not merely listen to the word, and so deceive yourselves. Do what is says." The gospel promotes the fundamental component of justice as one of its major dimensions. Our great end is liberty and justice for all; our indispensable means is faith in action.

Instead of doing what it says—loving God and loving others—Christians have too often expressed indifference or even hatred. When the Dalai Lama was invited to speak in the Washington National Cathedral, Christian groups in the United States launched a protest campaign—mentioning nothing about the underlying suffering of the people in Tibet. There are indeed profound theological differences between Christianity and Buddhism, and certainly if the Dalai Lama were invited to conduct a religious ceremony within a specifically Christian context, there would be justifiable concerns about the synchronistic theology of his hosts.

But the manner in which we express those concerns, and the way we relate to other religious groups that are being oppressed, is of critical importance. Shouldn't we be confident enough in our own faith to allay any fear about welcoming a leader of another persuasion to share a platform in order to promote religious freedom, mutual respect, and global justice? At a time when extremists of all faiths are screaming invectives against one another, it is our contention that Christian leaders have a unique responsibility to rise to the occasion and find common ground with those who have a shared concern for justice. That does not mean that we shrink from proclaiming the truth about Christ or water down our essential message, but it does signify that we should treat one another with the grace and love that Christ himself extended to others.

Christians, and especially evangelicals, have for too long oversimplified the problems of the world by claiming that if we just deal with personal sin, the world will be changed "automatically," as a matter of course. In other words, if we can only get people to accept Jesus Christ, everything else in their lives and societies will fall into place. This view completely negates the principles of the intentional action that is needed to bring about both personal and societal transformation. It negates what following Christ really means.

This view also represents an incomplete understanding of another truth. It is simplistic in that it essentially denies the presence and nature of evil. Evil is present in the world not only in our individual hearts but also in structures and systems designed to oppress, degrade, abuse, and kill others. If we are not intentional about bringing change and transformation into both lives and societies, it will not happen. To love people is to act on their behalf.

John Perkins had this to say about evangelicals and the
American civil rights movement of the 1960s:

> One of the greatest tragedies of the civil rights
> movement is that evangelicals surrendered
> their leadership in the movement by default
> to those with either a bankrupt theology or no
> theology at all, simply because a vast majority
> of Bible-believing Christians ignored a
> great and crucial opportunity in history for
> genuine, ethical action. The evangelical
> church—whose basic theology is the same as
> mine—had not gone on to preach the whole
> Gospel.[1]

The fall of humanity described in the book of Genesis
deals both with the sin of humankind and the consequences
of sin. The first couple is told that they will suffer death and
be driven out of Eden, that their life from that point on will be
characterized by sweat, tears, pain, and thorns.

But God's response to the fall does not end there. God
goes on to confront Satan and the evil he has unleashed into
human history. God's sense of justice is fully engaged, and
he informs the enemy that he will be trampled upon by the
seed of Adam and Eve. God will not allow injustice and evil
to prevail.

---

1. John Perkins, *Let Justice Roll Down,* p. 103.

This is the grand vision of the kingdom of God as described in the Genesis account. Humanity's personal sin will be dealt with, as will all the forces of evil that have been loosed upon the world. What is more, the perpetrator of evil will ultimately be crushed.

The desire for justice arises out of God's compassion for men and women, who have been created in his own image. Although humanity must bear the full responsibility for its actions, God is fully aware that evil entered the world only after the first humans were tempted by the devil. The origin of evil has never been disregarded by God, and he is out to eradicate its source.

Our involvement in justice and human rights often takes us to the source of evil in the present world. We recognize that there are spiritual realities behind evil, as well as the reality that evil can be perpetrated by depraved structures, ideologies, and systems. The history of humanity is replete with the stories of degenerate men and women who have unleashed great destruction—the emperor Nero, Adolf Hitler, Idi Amin, and Pol Pot are just a few examples.

Godless secularism, violent religious extremism, and despotic dictatorships in our day are ideologies and systems that degrade human beings and bring about profound harm. Do the people of God have anything to do with combating this problem, with responding to individuals and structures bent upon carrying out this malevolence? Involvement in justice and human rights is one key way of fulfilling God's mission in this world.

Scripture could not be clearer as to where God stands on the issue of justice. In Isaiah 58:6–7, the prophet asks rhetorically,

> Is not this the kind of fasting I have chosen; to loose the chains of injustice and untie the cords of the yoke, to set the oppressed free and break every yoke? Is it not to share your food with the hungry and to provide the poor wanderer with shelter—when you see the naked, to clothe him, and not to turn away from your own flesh and blood?

Isaiah continues with the promise that if God's people would "do away with the yoke of oppression, with the pointing finger and malicious talk," and instead focus their energies on helping the hungry and oppressed,

> your light will rise in the darkness, and your night will become like the noonday. The Lord will guide you always; he will satisfy your needs in a sun-scorched land and will strengthen your frame. You will be like a well-watered garden, like a spring whose waters never fail. Your people will rebuild the ancient ruins and will raise up the age-old foundations; you will be called Repairer

of Broken Walls, Restorer of Streets With Dwellings.[2]

In Isaiah 1:17, the prophet directs us to "seek justice, encourage the oppressed, defend the cause of the fatherless, plead the case of the widow." And in Amos 5:21–24, the Lord proclaims, "I hate, I despise your religious feasts; I cannot stand your assemblies." He adjures his people instead to "let justice roll on like a river, righteousness like a never-failing stream." In Micah 6:8 the prophetic message is reinforced:

He has showed you, O man, what is good.
And what does the Lord require of you?
To act justly and to love mercy and to walk
humbly with your God.

In *The Jesus I Never Knew*, author Philip Yancey sums up the message in this way:

Jesus came, he told us, not to destroy life but that we may have it more abundantly, "life . . . to the full." Paradoxically, we get this abundant life in ways we may not have counted on. We get it by investing in others, by taking courageous stands for justice, by ministering to the weak and needy, by pursuing God and

---

2. Isaiah 58:9–12.

not self. . . . Those who hunger and thirst for righteousness get filled.[3]

Christianity is clear that salvation is independent of our works. Nothing we do can earn us salvation. Our eternal destiny depends solely on the sacrifice of Jesus Christ, the Son of God, on the cross at Calvary, where he vicariously atoned for our sins through his death. Our *response* to that free gift of salvation determines our fate. And a natural reflection of our new life in Christ, once we have accepted him into our hearts, is a desire to follow his commands, to act as his disciples. So while working for justice is not by itself a precondition for salvation or entrance into the kingdom, it is an expected outcome, an indication, a sign. If, despite calling ourselves "Christian," we are completely devoid of compassion for the oppressed, the use of that label may be highly questionable.

If we are concerned, but our interest is limited to the "Christian" oppressed, we have missed the point entirely and are no better than the Pharisees of Jesus' day. It is not only a biblical command to speak out for all the oppressed but a conditional element of the Great Commission—for how can we hope that the nations will see the love of Jesus if we are unwilling to extend a hand of love and compassion to them? In addition, such action is in our own self-interest, for if we speak out for others they will be more likely to take notice of

---

3. Philip Yancey, *The Jesus I Never Knew*, p. 125.

Christian persecution. The words of Pastor Niemoller in Nazi
Germany are relevant here:

> *First they came for the Jews,*
> *And I did not speak out—*
> *Because I was not a Jew.*
> *Then they came for the communists*
> *And I did not speak out—*
> *Because I was not a communist.*
> *Then they came for the trade unionists—*
> *And I did not speak out—*
> *Because I was not a trade unionist.*
> *And then they came for me—*
> *And there was no one left*
> *To speak out for me.*[4]

But how do we attain such compassion, such a drive for
justice? We receive it from God, through the Holy Spirit.
Henri Nouwen expresses it this way:

> Compassion, to be with others when and
> where they suffer and to willingly enter
> into a fellowship of the weak, is God's way
> to justice and peace among people. Is this
> possible? Yes it is, but only when we dare

---

4. Pastor Martin Niemoller (1892–1984), Wikipedia.

to live with the radical faith that we do not
have to compete for love, but that love is
freely given to us by the One who calls us to
compassion.[5]

When we are filled with the Spirit of God, we are equipped
for his purposes with his compassion and his outrage at
injustice. If we claim to be Spirit-filled but lack a burning
desire for justice, all we really have is an experiential merry-
go-round, a self-indulgent emotionalism. And if our Christian
journey involves no more than bouncing from one charismatic
conference to the next, engaging in prayer and requesting
healing week after week with little transformation, we are
abusing the outpouring of the Holy Spirit. God gives us his
Spirit for a purpose—so that we will bear fruit, because we
are equipped to do his work.

A Christian approach to human rights is distinguished by
love. It is not simply about a cause, a political movement,
a philosophy—it is about human relationships, love, and
dignity. As Philip Yancey writes,

A political movement by nature draws lines,
makes distinctions, pronounces judgment;
in contrast, Jesus' love cuts across lines,
transcends distinctions and dispenses grace.
Regardless of the merits of a given issue

---

5. Henri Nouwen, *Here and Now: Living in the Spirit*, p. 99.

. . . political movements risk pulling onto themselves the mantle of power that smothers love. From Jesus I learn that, whatever activism I get involved in, it must not drive out love and humility, or otherwise I betray the kingdom of heaven.[6]

When Christians behave badly, with hatred or vengeance or evil, they tear away at the very fabric of the kingdom. But they also rend that fabric when they stand in silence, failing to act. We owe it to Christ and to humankind to take as part of our Christian mandate the principles expressed in the following song:

*I will speak out for those who have no
    voices.
I will stand up for the rights of all the
    oppressed.
I will speak truth and justice.
I'll defend the poor and the needy.
I will lift up the weak in Jesus' name.*

*I will speak out for those who have no
    choices.
I will cry out for those who live without
    love.
I will show God's compassion*

---

6. Ibid., p. 245.

To the crushed and broken in spirit.
I will lift up the weak in Jesus' name.[7]

Ultimately, however, we have long ago been assured that we are on the winning side. Injustice will in the end be defeated. Selwyn Hughes has said, "Those who live by evil shall perish by evil. Evil has the smell of death upon it. It may prosper for a time but its end is certain."[8] To hasten its demise, we as Christ's ambassadors must be more willing than we have been so far to cross borders—geographical, spiritual, political, and social—to throw wide the doors to allow the spirit of freedom, the spirit of life, to flow throughout our world.

---

7. Dave Bankhead, Sue Rinaldi, Ray Goudie and Steve Bassett. Word's Spirit of Praise Music/Admin. By CopyCare, 1990.

8. Selwyn Hughes, *Every Day With Jesus.*

BIBLIOGRAPHY

David Alton, *Signs of Contradiction: Twelve Outstanding People Who Changed Our World*, Hodder and Stoughton, 1996.

Valeri Barinov and Danny Smith, *Jailhouse Rock*, Hodder & Stoughton, 1990.

Susan Bergman, *A Cloud of Witnesses: 20th Century Martyrs*, HarperCollins, 1997.

Cal Bombay, *Let My People Go: The True Story of Present-Day Persecution and Slavery*, Multnomah, 1998.

Dietrich Bonhoeffer, *Letters and Papers from Prison*, SCM Press, 1953.

Steve Chalke and Alan Mann, *The Lost Message of Jesus*, Zondervan, 2003.

Tim Chester (Editor), *Justice, Mercy & Humility: Integral Mission and the Poor*, Paternoster Press, 2002.

Eileen Egan and Kathleen Egan, *Mother Teresa: Living the Word*, Image Books, 1989.

John Eldredge, *Waking the Dead,* Thomas Nelson, 2003.

Os Guinness, *Character Counts: Leadership Qualities in Washington, Wilberforce, Lincoln and Solzhenitsyn*, The Trinity Forum, 1999.

Os Guinness, *Unspeakable: Facing Up to Evil in an Age of Genocide and Terror*, HarperCollins, 2005.

Gary Haugen, *Good News About Injustice: A Witness of Courage in a Hurting World*, InterVarsity Press, 1999.

Nico Horn, *From Human Rights to Human Wrongs: The Dramatic Round-About-Turn of the South African Pentecostal Movement on Human Rights Issues,* Birmingham, November 2004.

Paul Kengor, *God and Ronald Reagan: A Spiritual Life*, HarperCollins, 2004.

Henri Nouwen, *Here and Now: Living in the Spirit*, Crossroad, 1994.

Samantha Power, *A Problem from Hell: America in the Age of Genocide*, Basic Books, 2002.

Geoffrey Robertson, *Crimes Against Humanity: The Struggle for Global Justice,* Penguin, 2nd Edition, 2002.

Benedict Rogers, *A Land Without Evil: Stopping the Genocide of Burma's Karen People*, Monarch, 2004.

Andrew Sinclair, *Che Guevara*, Sutton, 1998.

Danny Smith, *Lost Hero: Raoul Wallenberg's Dramatic Quest to Save the Jews of Hungary*, HarperCollins, 2001.

Danny Smith, *Who Says You Can't Change the World: Jubilee Campaign—Challenging Injustice*, Spring Harvest Publishing Division & Authentic Lifestyle, 2003.

John Stott, *The Incomparable Christ*, InterVarsity Press, 2001.

John Stott, *New Issues Facing Christians Today*, Zondervan, 1999.

Anna Lee Stangl, *Tried by Fire*, Monarch, 2003.

Howard Taylor, *Human Rights: Its Culture and Moral Confusions*, Rutherford House, 2004.

Corrie Ten Boom, *The Hiding Place*, Bantam Books, 1971.

J. R. R. Tolkien, *The Lord of the Rings*, HarperCollins, 1995.

George Verwer, *Out of the Comfort Zone*, OM Books, 2000.

Elie Wiesel, *Night*, Hill & Wang, 1960.

Philip Yancey, *The Jesus I Never Knew*, Zondervan, 1995.

Samuel Zalanga, *Christianity & Human Rights: A Sociological Assessment of the Rise of the Religious Right in America and the Consequences of That on Human Rights Concerns in the US and the Third World*, prepared for the Fourth Annual Lilly Fellows Program, Bethel University, November 11–14, 2004.

JUSTICE ORGANIZATIONS

CHRISTIAN

Christian Solidarity Worldwide (CSW)

www.csw.org.uk

www.cswusa.com

www.csw.org.hk

www.cswoz.org

Jubilee Campaign

www.jubileecampaign.co.uk

www.jubileecampaign.org

Open Doors

www.opendoors.org

International Christian Concern

www.persecution.org

International Justice Mission

www.ijm.org

Generosity Without Borders

www.generositywithoutborders.org

All India Christian Council

www.aiccindia.org

Dalit Freedom Network

www.dalitnetwork.org

Christians Concerned for Burma

www.prayforburma.org

SECULAR

Amnesty International

www.amnesty.org

Dalit Freedom Network

www.dalitnetwork.org

Human Rights Watch

www.hrw.org

Sow Hope

www.sowhope.org

ACKNOWLEDGEMENTS

Joseph D'souza provided information and illustrations from India, and Benedict Rogers furnished scenarios from East Timor, Burma, Pakistan, and Sri Lanka. Stories from Sudan, Indonesia, and Nagorno Karabakh were provided to the authors by Baroness Cox, and depictions of situations from other countries, such as North Korea, China, Laos, Peru, and Brazil have been drawn from a variety of sources, including Christian Solidarity Worldwide, Jubilee Campaign, and Lord Alton. A full list of books and publications to which the authors referred may be found in the bibliography. Stories and examples that are not footnoted were drawn from the authors' personal travel experiences. All other sources are referenced in footnotes.

The authors express their appreciation to Rosemary Morris and Mrs. K. Lajja of OM India for their assistance in this project, as well as to colleagues in Christian Solidarity Worldwide and the Dalit Freedom Network for their support.

ABOUT THE
AUTHORS

Dr. Joseph D'souza is founder and president of the All India Christian Council (AICC). Established in 1998, the AICC is one of the largest interdenominational coalitions of Christians that deals with national and human rights issues. The Council proactively addresses the persecution and oppression of Christians and other minorities in India.

Dr. D'souza is also international president of the Dalit Freedom Network whose mission is to empower the Dalits in their quest for human dignity, economic development, and socio-spiritual freedom. He helped found the organization based in the United States in 2002. The Dalit Freedom

Network now has offices in Canada, the UK, and Sweden and partners in over twenty-five nations.

In addition, Dr. D'souza serves as one of two vice presidents of Operation Mobilization (OM), an international movement that aims to transform lives and change communities by mobilizing and equipping people to share Christ's love and bring hope to the world.

For nearly twenty-five years, Dr. D'souza has been writing articles and speaking publicly on behalf of the poor and oppressed. In India, he has addressed over 100,000 people during many public meetings of on the issues of justice, human rights, and religious freedom. In 2005, Dr. D'souza published his first book, *Dalit Freedom Now and Forever*, which traces the history of the Dalit quest for emancipation and the response of the Indian church. It gives a strong challenge to eliminate caste discrimination around the world. An international best-seller, *Dalit Freedom Now and Forever* is now being translated into German and Spanish.

Dr. D'souza's articles have been published in major journals and magazines and have been included in several collections, such as *Communication in an Asian Context* and the recently published *Slavery: Now and Then* edited by Danny Smith of Jubilee Campaign. He has also presented papers at several national and international conferences on leadership development. He has been interviewed and quoted on Dalit and religious freedom issues by major national and international print and broadcast media including the BBC,

CNN, Asian News Service, and National Public Radio in the USA.

Dr. D'souza holds a B.S. in chemistry from Karnataka University, as well as an M.A. in communications from the Asian Theological Seminary in the Philippines. He was conferred with a Doctorate in Divinity degree from the Gospel for Asia Biblical Seminary, affiliated with Serampore University.

Benedict Rogers is a journalist and human rights advocate, as well as the author of *A Land Without Evil: Stopping the Genocide of Burma's Karen People* (Monarch, 2004). He works with the international human rights organization Christian Solidarity Worldwide (CSW) in London, where he is charged with responsibility for South Asia. He has also served as special adviser to the special representative of the United Kingdom's Foreign and Commonwealth Office Freedom of Religion Panel.

Benedict Rogers has traveled extensively on human rights fact-finding missions to Burma, East Timor, China, India, Pakistan, Sri Lanka, Armenia, and Nagorno Karabakh and has contributed to a variety of Christian and secular publications, including *Christianity Today, Crisis, Sojourners, Catholic Herald, Tablet, the Baptist Times, Forum 18, Asian Wall Street Journal, Hong Kong Standard, Irrawaddy, Times, Sunday Times,* and *Daily Telegraph.* He is coauthor of *The Life & Death of a Dotcom in China* (Asia Law & Practice Books,

2000), *New Ground: Engaging People with the Conservative Party through a Bold, Principled and Imaginative Foreign Policy*, and several other books and pamphlets. He contributed a chapter to *Slavery Now and Then*, edited by Danny Smith. Mr. Rogers, who has lived in Hong Kong, China, East Timor, Washington, D.C., and now London, holds a B.A. in Modern History, Economic History and Politics from the University of London, as well as an M.A in China Studies from the School of Oriental and African Studies, University of London. He wrote his M.A. dissertation on the policies of the Chinese government toward Christianity.

Benedict Rogers founded CSW UK's youth section, served as a member of the Board of Trustees of CSW UK, founded CSW Hong Kong and established CSW USA's Washington, D.C., organization. He is a Trustee of HART (the Humanitarian Aid Relief Trust), and previously the Metta Trust for Children's Education, as well as a member of the panel of advisers to Generositywithoutborders.org. He has appeared regularly on radio and television and briefs members of the British Parliament, the Foreign and Commonwealth Office, the European Union, the UN Commission on Human Rights, the US State Department, and the US Congress on issues relating to human rights and religious freedom. Mr. Rogers has spoken at the White House Christian Fellowship, the US Congressional "Faith and Law" Fellowship, the European Parliament, the Heritage Foundation, the Veritas Forum at New York and Columbia Universities, Yale University, the Conservative Party Conference, the International Christian Human Rights Conference, and the International Day of

Prayer for the Persecuted Church, as well as in churches, conferences, universities, and demonstrations around the world. In 2005 he was the Conservative Party's candidate for the city of Durham in the general election in the UK. Benedict Rogers also serves as vice-chairman of the Conservative Party Human Rights Commission.

Timothy J. Beals owns Credo Communications, LLC, a company that works with Christian ministry leaders and publishers to develop life-changing books, Bible-related products, and other Christian resources.

Prior to starting Credo Communications, LLC, Tim served as founder and publisher of World Vision Press. Tim also serves as Adjunct Professor of Writing at Cornerstone University (Grand Rapids, MI) and as Instructor of Publishing at University of the Nations (Kona, HI).

Tim is editor of *The Essential Ted W. Engstrom: Leader to Leaders* (Authentic) and editor of two Bible editions: *When You Pray* (Crossway) and *The Stewardship Resource Bible* (Crossway).

Tim is the editor of scores of books and Bibles and author of hundreds of local newspaper articles, national magazine features, and devotional pieces.

To respond to what you have read, please complete this form and send it either to Christian Solidarity Worldwide in the UK or to the All India Christian Council in India, and they will provide further information on how to get involved.

Name ....

Address ....

....

....

Email ....

I am interested in:

___ The work of CSW

___ The work of the All India Christian Council

___ The work of the Dalit Freedom Network

Specific countries/issues (please name)

....

....

....

CHRISTIAN SOLIDARITY WORLDWIDE
PO Box 99, New Malden, Surrey KT3 3YF, United Kingdom, admin@csw.org.uk
+44 845 456 5464 (UK 0845 456 5464)
FAX (Admin enquiries) +44 20 8942 8821 (UK 0208 942 8821)

ALL INDIA CHRISTIAN COUNCIL
Post Box No. 2174, Secunderabad, AP 500 003, India, administrator@aiccindia.org